THE EVOLUTION

OF

INTIMACY

THE EVOLUTION OF INTIMACY

TOWARDS A NEW POLITICS OF LOVE

YOUR UNIQUE, CLARIFIED DESIRE IS THE DESIRE OF REALITY ITSELF

. . .

From Conscious Evolution 1.0 to Conscious Evolution 2.0

One Mountain, Many Paths: Oral Essays Volume Eleven

DR. MARC GAFNI AND BARBARA MARX HUBBARD

Author: Marc Gafni and Barbara Marx Hubbard
Title: The Evolution of Intimacy
From Conscious Evolution 1.0 to Conscious Evolution 2.0

Identifiers: ISBN 979-8-88834-043-1 (electronic)
ISBN 979-8-88834-047-9 (paperback)

Edited by Timothy Paul Aryeh, Paul Bennett, Dorothea Betz, and David Cicerchi

World Philosophy and Religion Press, St. Johnsbury, VT
in conjunction with

IP Integral Publishers

https://worldphilosophyandreligion.org

JOIN THE REVOLUTION!

CONTENTS

CHAPTER THREE   **MY UNIQUE DESIRE IS GOD'S DESIRE:
HEALING THE CRISIS OF DESIRE**

CHAPTER FOUR   **HEALING THE CRISIS OF INTIMACY:
FALLING MADLY IN LOVE
WITH OURSELVES AS UNIQUE
CONFIGURATIONS OF DESIRE AND
INTIMACY**

CHAPTER FIVE   **CRISIS IS AN EVOLUTIONARY DRIVER:
OUR COLLECTIVE AWAKENING TO
REALITY MADLY IN LOVE WITH US**

EDITORIAL NOTE ABOUT AUTHORSHIP, EDITING, AND THE RADICAL CONTEXT FOR THIS SERIES

ORAL ESSAYS FROM THE ONE MOUNTAIN, MANY PATHS WEEKLY BROADCAST

This volume is part of the Oral Essays library, a series of lightly edited, compiled transcripts of oral teachings given by Dr. Marc Gafni and the late Barbara Marx Hubbard in their weekly online broadcast, *One Mountain, Many Paths,* which they co-founded in 2017. Originally called an "Evolutionary Church," *One Mountain, Many Paths* became a key venue for the articulation of an inspired and deeply grounded new Story of Value in response to the meta-crisis. Marc and Barbara—together with Zak Stein,[1] Kristina Kincaid, Ken Wilber, Sally Kempton, Lori Galperin, Aubrey Marcus and dozens of other thought-leaders over the years—began to articulate what they call a World Philosophy and World Religion[2] as a context for our diversity.

---

1   Zak, together with Ken Wilber, has been Marc's primary intellectual partner and an initiate lineage holder in CosmoErotic Humanism.

2   This project is grounded in four core organizational frameworks: 1) The Center for World Philosophy and Religion, co-founded by Marc Gafni, Zachary Stein, Sally Kempton, and Ken Wilber, and chaired over the years by John P. Mackey, Barbara Marx Hubbard, Aubrey Marcus, Gabrielle Anwar and Shareef Malnik, Carrie Kish and Adam Bellow, and Kathleen J. Brownback. 2) The Office for the Future, chaired by Stephanie Valcke and Ivan Bossyut. 3) The World Philosophy and Religion Press, founded and chaired by Aubrey Marcus, together with Marc Gafni and Zachary Stein. 4) The Foundation for Conscious Evolution, founded

Until Barbara's passing in 2019, she and Marc transmitted teachings together as evolutionary partners and "whole mates," weaving together insights and transmissions from their decades of practice, study, teaching, and activism into a synergy of wisdom, a grounded vision for future policy across all sectors of society.

Much of the *Dharma* material below comes directly from Marc, so it was originally all in quotation marks—but that looked a little odd. So per his suggestion we removed them, and the reader should consider the paragraphs on the next several pages as one extended quote from him. We are joyfully grateful to Marc for the clarity of his *Dharma*, the elegance and "second simplicity" of this language, and the mad, Outrageous Love with which he transmits his teachings.

Barbara and Marc called the mission of *One Mountain* "a Planetary Awakening in Evolutionary Love Through Unique Self Symphonies." We are an evolutionary community with a deeply grounded, radically alive, and "post-tragic" revolutionary spirit. We are activating a new humanity and awakening as a new species: *Homo amor*, the fulfillment of *Homo sapiens*.

One Mountain is committed to articulating a Story of Value that can become the ground for the new society that must be birthed in response to the meta-crisis. We recognize that we are living at a pivotal moment in history. In this "time between stories," the great moral imperative is to tell the new Story of Value. It is ours to do, personally and collectively, with great trembling and ecstatic joy.

FROM DOGMA TO *DHARMA*: ETERNAL AND EVOLVING FIRST PRINCIPLES AND FIRST VALUES

The teachings are grounded in decades of deep study across many wisdom traditions. Over the years, week by week, these teachings were

by Barbara Marx Hubbard and currently chaired by Peter Fiekowsky. For a complete list of key leadership, see the Office for the Future website, www.officeforthefuture.com.

incrementally developed within the framework of the *One Mountain, Many Paths* broadcast. We often refer to these teachings as *Dharma*.

This word was originally used in lineage traditions to refer to something like universal law. This is a crucial realization: just as there is universal law in mathematical value, there is also a sense of universal law in ethics and value.

Historically, *Dharma* often devolved into unchanging dogma. Evolution was ignored, and the natural process of *Dharma* evolution became disconnected from its deep, eternal context. The weakness of the word *Dharma* is that too often it did not include the evolving insights of the sciences, it confused local cultural truths with universal truths, and it used words like "eternal," as in "eternal Tao," as opposed to words like "evolution."

Eternal came to mean unchanging, and that kind of thinking often led to overly ethnocentric readings of *Dharma*. Local systems would claim their religious and cultural insights as immutable, which stood in the way of the emergence of a genuine world Story of Value that is real, inherent to Cosmos, and backed by the Universe—even as it is also always evolving.

Or, as we often say, "eternal value is evolving value. The eternal Tao is the evolving Tao."

We have shown that, emergent from profound insights in the "interior sciences," eternal does not mean unchanging in time; it means what we call the deeper Field of ErosValue that is beneath culture, geography, and history, which lives beneath all individual and collective values, and beneath time and space itself.

As such, we have gradually transitioned from the term *Dharma* to the term *Value*, in the sense of the Field of Value that lives beneath all values. This Field of Value discloses as First Principles and First Values embedded in a Story of Value.

Indeed, as the interior sciences knew and the exterior sciences imply, Reality arises in a Field of ErosValue in which an entire set of mathematical, musical, molecular, moral, and mystical values are the very ground of all being. That Field of Value is eternal—the true ground of the Good, True and Beautiful—even as it is evolving.

But of course, it is equally critical not just to talk about evolving value, but to ground the evolving value in its true nature, the eternal Field of First Principles and First Values, always reaching for ever-more life, ever-more love, ever-more care, ever-more depth, ever-more uniqueness, ever-more intimate communion, and ever-more transformation.

As such, when we refer to the word *Dharma*, which still appears in these texts together with the word value, we refer to an evolving *Dharma* grounded in an *eternal and evolving* Field of Value. Indeed, eternity and evolution are two faces of the whole, opposites joined at the hip, that characterize the nature of our Cosmos in virtually all of its expressions.

It's in these terms that we ground a robust world philosophy that integrates the validated, leading-edge insights of premodern traditional wisdom, modern wisdom, and more recent postmodern insights, weaving them together into a new whole greater than the sum of its parts.

This new whole is a shared Story of Value rooted in First Principles and First Values that are both eternal and evolving.

These First Principles and First Values of Cosmos are woven together into a new Story of Value as a context for our diversity, a new Universe Story. This new Story gives us the best possible responses we have to the mystery, and to the great questions:

- Who am I? Who are we?
- Where am I? Where are we?
- What should I do? What should we do?

It is only through such a shared Universe Story—a narrative of identity and ethos as a context for our blessed diversity—that we can realize how what unites is so much greater than what divides us.

Only a new Story of Value will allow us to both respond to the meta-crisis and participate together in birthing the most true, good, and beautiful world that we already know is possible.

THIS ORAL ESSAYS SERIES IS AN ENTRYWAY TO THE GREAT LIBRARY OF COSMOEROTIC HUMANISM

This Oral Essays series is part of the overarching project of the Great Library at the Center for World Philosophy and Religion, led by Dr. Marc Gafni, together with Dr. Zak Stein. The aim of the Great Library project is to articulate a robust and comprehensive new Story of Value, CosmoErotic Humanism, in the form of dozens of well-researched and extensively footnoted academic works.

Our vision is to provide the philosophical framework that will be vital for navigating humanity through this time of immense crisis and transformation.

To begin your journey into CosmoErotic Humanism, we tenderly refer you to the book *First Principles and First Values*, co-authored by Marc Gafni, Zak Stein, and Ken Wilber, under the name David J. Temple. David J. Temple is a pseudonym created for enabling ongoing collaborative authorship at the Center for World Philosophy and Religion. The two primary authors behind David J. Temple are Marc Gafni and Zak Stein, and for different projects, specific writers will be named as part of the collaboration, such as Ken Wilber and others.

Three other volumes complete this introduction: *A Return to Eros*, by Marc Gafni and Kristina Kincaid; *Your Unique Self*, by Marc Gafni; and *Education in a Time between Worlds*, by Zak Stein.

We hope that the Oral Essays in this volume, with their informal style of transmission, will serve as an allurement and entryway for you into the more formal books of the Great Library that provide the robust intellectual underpinnings of the new Story of Value.

A NOTE ABOUT THE EDITORS

This Oral Essays collection has been edited by students of the new Story of CosmoErotic Humanism. Each of us has actively participated in *One Mountain, Many Paths*, and most of us have been in deep "Holy of Holies" study with Dr. Marc Gafni for many years.

We have been privileged to find ourselves well-versed in the teachings, and even emerging as lineage-holders of CosmoErotic Humanism.[3]

We view this editing project as a privilege and a deep practice of study and clarification. We experience ourselves as a *mystical editing society*, frequently meeting and conversing together about the content—the depth of knowledge and wisdom offered here—as well as the technical intricacies involved with publishing a beautiful and coherent series of books. In so doing, we function as a "Unique Self Symphony," which itself is a Dharmic

---

3   CosmoErotic Humanism is a world philosophical movement aimed at reconstructing the collapse of value at the core of global culture. Much like Romanticism or Existentialism, CosmoErotic Humanism is not merely a theory but a movement that changes the very mood of Reality. It is an invitation to participate in evolving the source code of consciousness and culture towards a cosmocentric *ethos* for a planetary civilization.

The term CosmoErotic Humanism, initially coined by Dr. Gafni and colleagues, points to a complex, multi-faceted, layered, and nuanced evolutionary set of insights that has evolved over decades of intensive research, teaching, and spiritual practice from deep within a wide range of wisdom traditions (including the Wisdom of Solomon lineage tradition, Bodhisattva Buddhism, and Kashmir Shaivism), as well as multiple disciplines including complexity theory, chaos theory, emergence theory, molecular biology, and the more classical disciplines of the humanities.

The seeds of CosmoErotic Humanism were planted with Dr. Marc Gafni's work on a two-volume, 1,000-page opus called *Radical Kabbalah* (Integral Publishers, 2012). This scholarly work, sourced from deep study within the esoteric lineage texts of the Wisdom of Solomon, points to a non-dual, or acosmic, realization which—unlike the prevailing conceptualization of non-duality—does not efface the human being; rather, it is highly humanistic in its nature. The next step in the evolution of CosmoErotic Humanism was the insight that all of Reality is evolving Eros, which lives in, as, and through the human being. A failure of Eros leads inexorably to the creation of narratives of "pseudo-eros." CosmoErotic Humanism is a response to the modern mental and social breakdown sourced in the proliferation of multiple forms of pseudo-eros and its broken narratives, such as rivalrous conflict governed by win/lose metrics and the dogmatic denial of intrinsic value in Cosmos, which together generate our current "global intimacy disorder."

term that connotes an omni-considerate collaboration between realized Unique Selves synergizing our unique gifts into a new emergence greater than the sum of the parts. Even as we worked diligently to standardize our editing styles, meeting on a weekly basis to debate the nuances of phrasing, we also operated from within a deep appreciation of the unique style that each editor brought to his or her work. As such, the reader might notice some variation in editing style among the books.

Please note that Dr. Marc Gafni has not reviewed these edited Oral Essays, as he is deeply engaged in writing the formal books of the Great Library. But he has been generous in responding to questions and providing overall guidance in the project. Overall, as Marc's students and students of the *Dharma*, we have made it a key project at the Center to publish these pieces of work relatively independently.

OUR UNIQUE ORAL-ESSAY EDITING STYLE PRESERVES THE ENERGY OF THE ORIGINAL TRANSMISSION

Dr. Marc Gafni is a uniquely gifted teacher whose oral transmission is imbued with a quality that has proven transformative for his students. Many of us feel mystically transformed by both the content and the underlying energy of the transmission style. Therefore, as we like to say, *trust the magic ways the Dharma comes through your unique understanding!*

As Marc's empowered students, colleagues, and beloved friends, we have a deep knowing that these teachings are vital for the survival and thriving of humanity as we know it, and we recognize the importance of publishing his teachings in a written format that will be accessible by future generations. At the same time, we sought to preserve the Eros of the original oral transmission with all of its nuance, power, and depth. Our intention in the editing process, to the greatest extent possible, has been to keep these spoken artifacts intact in order to maintain the flow of the original transmission. We have therefore chosen not to engage in intensive formal editing, as we found that doing so resulted in the loss of the energetic transmission that is so key to fully receiving the *Dharma*.

After experimenting with many ways to present these texts, we developed a specific way of laying out the text on the page. Marc, in collaboration with Zak Stein and Russian intellectual/artist Elena Maslova-Levin—and ultimately all of the editors, through many conversations—developed a unique, artistic presentation of the text, using bolding, italics, bullet points, and other stylistic features which together serve to accentuate the immediacy of the oral transmission.

As part of this editing style, intended to preserve the integrity of the original transmission, we have refrained from removing the frequent recapitulations of key themes. We found that each recapitulation contributes something vital to the rhythm and music beneath the words, like the beating drum of our hearts. These recapitulations not only review previous material but also add important new emphases, perspectives, and elements of the new Story of Value. We ask for your patience as a reader to trust the rhythm of these texts, and we trust you as a reader to have the depth and steadiness to find your way through.

KEY COMPONENTS: LINK TO THE ORIGINAL BROADCAST, EVOLUTIONARY LOVE CODES AND PRAYER

To supplement the written word, each episode includes a QR code linking to the original broadcast on YouTube, as well as occasional links to featured songs and video clips.

Each episode also centers around an "Evolutionary Love Code," formulated by Marc. These codes are part of the ongoing articulation and distillation of the *Dharma* as it unfolds and emerges, week by week, over the course of many years, through the mystical process we call Outrageous Love or Evolutionary Love.

Another core component of the *One Mountain, Many Paths* episodes is what Marc and Barbara called "Evolutionary Prayer." Prayer is experienced in *One Mountain* not in the old fundamentalist sense of a "cosmic vending-machine god" who is alienated from Cosmos. Marc refers to this as the "god you do not and should not believe in"—and he often adds, "the god you don't believe in does not exist."

GOD IS THE INFINITE INTIMATE

In fact, in the *Dharma* of CosmoErotic Humanism, a new name for God has emerged: the "Infinite Intimate," who appears in first-, second-, and third-person expressions. Marc first shared this name as he heard it whispered in 2023, although earlier intimations and formulations of the name appeared as early as 2010.

In first person, God is infinitely alive and as intimate as our own first-person experience.

In second person, God is the infinitely intimate Personhood of Cosmos that knows our name and holds us—the God about whom we say, *whenever we fall, we fall into Her hands.* This is the God who is our Beloved, Father, Mother, Lover, and Evolutionary Partner.

Finally, in third person, God inheres in all of the First Principles and First Values of Cosmos, and in the laws of science (both interior and exterior) that govern manifest Reality.

Therefore, we have a realization of God as not only the Infinity of Power but also the Infinity of Intimacy.

In *One Mountain, Many Paths*, we are reclaiming prayer at a higher level of consciousness. And we are reclaiming prayer as deep, alive, loving, and intimate conversations with God as the Infinite Intimate who knows our name.

REFLECTING ON THE CO-CREATION BETWEEN
DR. MARC GAFNI AND BARBARA MARX HUBBARD

Barbara and Marc met five years before Barbara passed. As Barbara said so often, "before I met Marc, I was sure that I was done." Barbara had taught so beautifully for decades, focusing particularly on a powerful articulation of "conscious evolution." Indeed, it would not be inaccurate to say that Barbara was the greatest storyteller of conscious evolution of her time.

Conscious evolution was also a premise in Marc's thinking, but drawn from an entirely different set of sources and experiences. Barbara drew from the classical sources of evolutionary spirituality, such as Teilhard de Chardin, Buckminster Fuller, and many others. Indeed, she was closely associated with Fuller, and was perhaps de Chardin's most ardent intellectual devotee.

Marc drew a somewhat different vision of conscious evolution from the interior sciences of the great wisdom traditions, with a primary emphasis on what he refers to as the "Solomon lineages," merged together with careful readings of the leading edges of the sciences. In the old version of conscious evolution, the movement from unconscious to conscious was a movement of evolution by chance to evolution by choice.

Together Marc and Barbara evolved the old version of Conscious Evolution, pointing out that evolution itself was always in some sense conscious, but as Marc formulated it, the awakening to conscious evolution refers to the awakening of evolution as human consciousness, coupled with the human realization of being conscious evolution in person, and the human capacity to locate oneself within the context of the larger evolutionary story.

Marc focused his attention on an entirely different dimension of Reality, which he and his colleagues began to call CosmoErotic Humanism. The Intimate Universe, Homo amor, Unique Self and Unique Self Symphonies, God as the Infinity of Intimacy, Eros and the CosmoErotic Universe, distinctions like Role Mate, Soul Mate and Whole Mate, the Four Selves,

Evolutionary Love, Outrageous Love, Evolution: the Love Story of the Universe, First Principles and First Values, Evolving Perennialism, the Evolution of Love, and many more are terms articulated by Gafni and shared with Barbara in their conversation, study, and creative engagement.

Some terms they coined together, for example "a Planetary Awakening in Love through Unique Self Symphonies," where Gafni described Unique Self Symphonies, and Barbara aligned her vision of a planetary Pentecost to Marc's vision of Unique Self Symphonies.

Other key terms were unique and articulated by Barbara, for example: conscious evolution, teleros, telerotic, from joining genes to joining genius, regenopause, vocational arousal, birthing of humanity, synergy engine, and of course her work around what she called the Wheel of Co-creation.

Ultimately, Marc and Barbara attempted to synergize their work in what they called the Wheel of Co-creation 2.0. Barbara and Marc experienced themselves as merging their respective *Dharma* into what they began to refer to as Conscious Evolution 2.0, or later, CosmoErotic Humanism.

The first 129 episodes of One Mountain, Many Paths took place in the last period of Barbara's life and reflect the depth and texture of the stunning evolutionary whole-mate meeting between her and Marc. As Barbara was deep in study with Marc, a lot of what she shared in Evolutionary Church was the *Dharma* of their deep study and collaboration.

Although sometimes it may be clear who is speaking, we generally publish these early episodes in what we are calling "one voice." The first 129 episodes, with Marc and Barbara together, have been grouped chronologically. Episodes 130 to 400 and onwards, which were transmitted by Marc, have been grouped by topic.

THE INVITATION

We invite you to find your way into this revolution. Each one of our Unique Selves and unique gifts are desperately needed as we co-create this new Story of Value together, as part of the covenant between generations, for the sake of the whole.

Let's *play a larger game* and evolve the very source code of consciousness and culture together.

With mad love,

The Editors

LOVE OR DIE

LOCATING OURSELVES: ARTICULATING THE ESSENTIAL CONTEXT FOR THE ONE MOUNTAIN, MANY PATHS ORAL ESSAYS

SETTING OUR INTENTION

Intention setting is everything.

We're here—as da Vinci was with his cohort in the Renaissance—**to play a larger game, to participate in the evolution of love, which is to tell the new Story of Value rooted in First Principles and First Values.**

- Our intention is to recognize the critical historical juncture in which we find ourselves.
- Our intention is to take our seat at the table of history and to say, *we take responsibility for this.*
- Our intention is to participate as revolutionaries for the sake of the whole.

What we're here to do is revolution; revolution for the sake of the evolution of love.

It's a revolution for the sake of the trillions of unborn lives that will not manifest:

- The unborn loves
- The unborn creativity
- The unborn goodness
- The unborn truth
- The unborn beauty

All of it looks to us.

Not because we're engaged in grandiosity. Not at all!

- We're trembling before She.
- We're trembling with joy at the privilege.
- We're trembling with joy at the responsibility.
- We're trembling with joy at the Possibility of Possibility.
- We have to enact a new Story in this moment of time. Because it is only a new Story that can change the vector of history.

The most revolutionary act that we can do—the greatest moral imperative of this time—**is to articulate a new Story at this time between worlds and this time between stories.**

Story is not made up, as postmodernity suggests. **We all live in inescapable frameworks; our framework is the story we live in.** Right now, Reality lives according to win/lose metrics, a story that is generating existential risk. **We need to change that story.**

When we change that story, when we tell a new Story—not a made-up story, but a new Story of Value, rooted in First Principles and First Values—**then it all changes.**

We need to participate in the evolution of the source code of consciousness and culture, which is the evolution of love.

It's the most important, exciting, evolutionary, revolutionary act that we can do to alleviate suffering: to be lovers.

Like Rumi, the great poet of Sufism, we have to be "mad lovers," because it's the only sanity.

To be mad lovers is to see around the corner, to not be so obsessed with the details of the contractions of my life.

Let me see bigger.

Let me take complete care of myself in every possible way, let me completely attend to those in my circle of intimacy and influence, and then—*let me expand my circle.*

That's what we're here for.

- ◆ Our intention is to participate in the *LoveForce*, the *LoveIntelligence*, the *LoveBeauty*, the *LoveDesire* that literally animates Cosmos all the way up and all the way down.
- ◆ Our intention is to participate in the evolution of love.

[In the next few pages we will cover some key concepts which are essential to locating ourselves and setting the context for all the One Mountain, Many Paths Oral Essays. —Eds.]

OVERVIEW: EROS IS NO LONGER A LUXURY—IT'S LOVE OR DIE

Eros is life.

The failure of Eros destroys life.

Our lack of Eros is poised to destroy the world.

All civilizations have fallen because the stories that they lived in were, in some sense, stories based on rivalrous conflict governed by win/lose metrics. Every civilization was weakened by interior polarization caused by the lack of a shared Story of Value.

We now have a global civilization, but we haven't created a shared Story of Value.

We haven't solved the generator functions that caused all civilizations to fall. Our global civilization has exponential technologies and extraction models depleting the Earth of resources that took billions of years to create, which is going to lead to a civilizational collapse.

Existential risk is risk to our very existence.

The choice is clear: love or die.

It's that simple.

Eros is no longer a luxury. It is an absolute necessity for the survival of the individual and the planet.

In the last half a century, modern psychology has documented an age-old truth: a fully nourished baby who is not held in loving arms will die.

So too, our world, both personal and global—even with all the resources of intelligence and technology at our disposal—will die without being held in love, in the embrace of Eros.

We must embrace a personal path of love and a global politics of love.

Not ordinary love. Not love which is "mere human sentiment," but Eros, or what we sometimes call Outrageous Love, which is the heart of existence itself.

We live in a world of outrageous pain.

The only response is Outrageous Love.

WHAT IS EROS?

Eros is the experience of radical aliveness, moving towards, seeking, desiring ever-deeper contact and ever-greater wholeness.[4] Eros is the core fabric of Reality's being and the motivational architecture of Reality's becoming.

Eros is what animates the evolutionary impulse itself, from the very inception of Cosmos all the way to our very selves, who awaken to the realization that the evolutionary impulse throbs uniquely in each of us.

The realization of human awakening and transformation that lies at the core of the interior sciences is the invitation—or even the urgent and desperate demand—of a madly loving Cosmos animated by infinities of power and infinities of intimacy.

The demand—the desperate invitation, the plea, the tender and fierce command of Cosmos that lives inside every human being—is to awaken: to awaken to our true nature as unique incarnations of Eros and Ethos that are needed and desperately desired by All-That-Is. Said slightly differently: Reality is Eros. Or: God is Eros.

The failure of Eros destroys life. The collapse of Eros is always the hidden (or not so hidden) root cause for the collapse of ethics.

This is true both personally and collectively. We live in a moment of a worldwide and personal collapse of Eros. Our lack of Eros is poised to de-

---

4 We define Eros through what we refer to as the Eros equation (one of a series of what we call interior science equations):

Eros = Radical Aliveness x *Desiring (Growing + Seeking)* x *Deeper Contact* x *Greater Wholeness* x *Self Actualization/Self Transcendence (Creation [Destruction])*

There are good reasons for the formal language of the interior science equations in these writings, and the reader is invited to explore them on their own, in particular, in our work, David J. Temple, *First Principles and First Values: Forty-Two Propositions on CosmoErotic Humanism, the Meta-Crisis, and the World to Come* (World Philosophy and Religion, 2024).

stroy the world. Humanity is currently experiencing what has come to be known as existential risk, a risk to our very existence, or what I will refer to as the Second Shock of Existence.

EXISTENTIAL RISK: THE SECOND SHOCK OF EXISTENCE

The first shock of existence is the death of the human being—the realization that we will die, which dawns in human consciousness at the beginning of history. We are not talking about the biological fact of death but the *existential* realization of death. Although the interior sciences disclose that death is a portal between two days (there is vast empirical,[5] philosophical,[6] and anthro-ontological evidence[7] for the continuity of consciousness[8]), death is also, in our own direct surface experience, a stark end. And that is obviously not a bug but a feature in the system.

---

5   We refer to evidence gathered by the most serious of researchers, beginning with Henry and Edith Sedgwick at Cambridge University and William James at Harvard University, and continuing in highly rigorous form for the last 150 years, as recapitulated by Whiteheadian scholar David Ray Griffin in multiple volumes. See also, for example, Dean Radin, *Real Magic: Unlocking Your Natural Psychic Abilities to Create Everyday Miracles* (Potter/TenSpeed/Harmony, 2018), *The Conscious Universe: The Scientific Truth of Psychic Phenomena* (HarperCollins, 2010), and other books. Or see the earlier classic by Frederic William Henry Myers, *Human Personality and Its Survival of Bodily Death* (Longmans, Green, 1907).

6   This requires a cogent analysis of materialism and dualism, and the introduction of the far more cogent third possibility which we have called "pan-interiority."

7   We discuss Anthro-Ontology in some depth in *First Principles and First Values*, and see also the fuller conversation in David J. Temple, *First Principles and First Values: Towards an Evolving Perennialism: Introducing the Anthro-Ontological Method*—both published by World Philosophy and Religion Press, in Conjunction with Integral Publishers. For now, we will simply define it as an "innate and clear interior gnosis directly available to the human being."

8   See Dr. Marc Gafni and Dr. Zachary Stein's essay in preparation, "Beyond Death: Anthro-Ontology, Philosophy, and Empiricism." This essay is slated to appear in the book *Towards a World Religion: Homo Amor Essays*. The essay is also the ground for a larger book by the same authors, *Twelve Portals to Life Beyond Death: Responding to the Second Shock of Existence,* in which we discuss three forms of material: the empirical, the philosophical, and the anthro-ontological, and show how each form discredits the notion of death as the end.

Our first-person experience is that death ends this life. It is not the *totality* of our experience if we go deeper inside, but it is obviously intended to be the central, potent, and painful dimension of every human life. Indeed, as Ernest Becker potently reminded us, the denial of death is at our peril.

All the stories and all the plotlines and all the threads of living end at that moment. Whatever happens beyond, we have an actual experience of ending. **Paradoxically, that ending, the experience of the finality of mortality, is what presses us into life.** From the implicit demand of the first shock of existence, human beings were activated and pressed into creative emergence, and what emerged was all of human culture, both interior and exterior.

The second shock of existence is the realization of the potential death of all humanity. After all the stages of human history—matter, life, and mind in all of their stages of evolutionary unfolding—we have come to this place in the evolution of humanity, in which the gap between our exponentially expanding exterior technologies and our stalled (or even regressing) interior technologies of value has created dire catastrophic and existential risks.

This gap generates extraction models and exponential growth curves, rivalrous conflicts based on win/lose metrics, tragedies of the commons, and multipolar traps, in which everyone has to keep producing to the nth degree, including weaponized exponential threats to our very existence because we are afraid that the other parties are going to do it and not be transparent—hide it from us and then dominate us.

GENERATOR FUNCTIONS FOR EXISTENTIAL RISK

Let's outline clearly the main *generator functions for existential risk*.

Rivalrous conflicts governed by zero-sum, win/lose metrics. Rivalrous conflicts generate extraction models at the core of the economic system and exponential growth curves. Both of these drive and are driven by a contrived system of artificially manufactured desires and needs, delivered into culture by ever more precise forms of micro-targeting to individuals and groups through the ever more immersive environment of the internet.

Next, rivalrous conflicts and exponential growth curves animated by win/lose metrics generate **complicated, fragile world systems** highly vulnerable to myriad forms of collapse. Fragile local systems are made exponentially more fragile on a global level by our inability to meet global challenges with social, legal, political, economic, and ethical infrastructures that remain largely local.

All of this is a direct result of the failure to develop more adequate interior technologies that would be sufficiently compelling to displace "rivalrous conflict governed by win/lose metrics" as the motivational architecture for the human life world.

This failure has led to the conditions that will cause the implosion of systems that are already and quite literally on the brink of collapsing themselves. That's what we mean by the *second shock of existence*.

To recapitulate: the second shock of existence is not the death of the human being, but the potential death of humanity.

It is the *Death Star* moment of our species.

THE DECONSTRUCTION OF INTRINSIC VALUE

We stand in this moment poised between utopia and dystopia, at a time between worlds and a time between stories. We need a new Story of Value, eternal yet evolving, rooted in First Principles and First Values, which would become a universal grammar of value and a context for our diversity.

This is exactly what the Renaissance was. It was a time between worlds and a time between stories. In the Renaissance, we had recently been challenged by the Black Death, a pandemic that swept across Europe. The Black Death destroyed between a third to half of Europe and a huge part of

Asia. People died horrifically, brutally, in the streets. They had no idea how to meet this challenge, and so, in response to the Black Death, da Vinci and Ficino and their cohorts understood that they had to tell a new Story of Value.

That story was the story of modernity. Did they get it right?

- They got part of it right, which birthed, to use Jürgen Habermas' phrase, "the dignities of modernity," such as new ways of gathering information and universal human rights.
- But they also deconstructed the source of Value. They lost the basis for the Good, the True, and the Beautiful.

The basis used to be divine revelation: *God told us.* But this claim was owned by religion, and every religion began to overreach and over-claim. The revelation was thus often mediated through cultural categories and wasn't fully accurate.

Modernity threw out revelation, but was unable to establish a new basis for value.

Value was just assumed to be real. As it says in the founding document of the American Revolution: *We hold these truths to be self-evident*—that is, *we don't really have a basis for value; we just take it as a given.*

In other words, modernity took out a loan of social capital from the traditional world. The source of value was never worked out.

And then, gradually, value began to collapse.

- The Universe Story began to collapse.
- The belief that the Good, the True, and the Beautiful are real began to collapse.
- The belief that Love is real began to collapse.

As Bertrand Russell is reported to have said, "I cannot see how to refute the arguments for the subjectivity of ethical values, but I find myself incapable of believing that all that is wrong with wanton cruelty is that I do not like it."

What do you do if you grew up in a world in which value is not real? A world without a source of value, without a Universe Story, without a story of human identity, without a story of desire, without a narrative of power?

In the words of W.B. Yeats, *the center does not hold.*

- You have a collapse at the very center of society, because you no longer have Eros.
- You no longer have a Reality in which value is real, and so you have this lingering sense of emptiness.
- You have a complete collapse at the very center.
- We become *the hollow men and the stuffed men*, gesture without form.

And that's the source of our current existential risk.

THE DEEPER ROOT CAUSE OF THE META-CRISIS: A GLOBAL INTIMACY DISORDER

Above, I have outlined the major generator functions of existential risk. But there is a deeper cause for the existential risk that lurks underneath the rivalrous conflict governed by win/lose metrics and the fragile systems they engender.

And we cannot take the Death Star down without discerning and addressing this. We have already alluded to this root cause above, but at this point we need to make it more explicit so that, from this context, the adequate root response will become clear.

Modernity threw out the revelation, but was unable to establish a new basis for value.

This ostensibly surprising statement can be understood in a few simple steps:

1. All of the catastrophic and existential risk challenges we face are global: from climate change to artificial intelligence, pandemics, systems collapse, and exponential arms races.
2. Every global challenge self-evidently requires a global solution.
3. Global solutions can only be implemented with global co-ordination.
4. Global co-ordination is impossible without global coherence.
5. Global coherence is only possible if there is a global resonance between the parts.
6. Global resonance is only possible if we have global intimacy.

ONLY A SHARED STORY OF VALUE CAN GENERATE GLOBAL INTIMACY

Global intimacy—just like intimacy in a couple—is only possible when there is a shared story.

Not just a shared history, but a shared Story of Value.

- It is only a shared global story that can generate a new emergent quality of intimacy: global intimacy.
- A shared Story of Value must be rooted in shared ordinating values, or what we have called evolving First Values and First Principles.
- Intimacy requires a shared grammar of value as a matrix for a shared Story of Value.

The global intimacy disorder is the root cause for existential risk. The global intimacy disorder underlies the core generator functions for existential risk.

The global intimacy disorder is rooted in the failure to experience ourselves in a field of shared intrinsic value. This failure derives from the deconstruction of value.

Indeed, it is wholly accurate to say that **the root cause of the two generator functions of existential risk is the failed story of intrinsic value, or what we might also call the breakdown of Eros.**

1. The first generator function is **the success story**. Our modern success story is rivalrous conflict governed by win/lose metrics, which violates all the terms of the Intimacy Equation: there is no shared identity and no mutuality of recognition, feeling, value or purpose, and instead of *relative* otherness, there is *alienated* otherness. Such a story generates complicated fragile systems with no allurement or intimacy between the parts, systems which optimize for efficiency (as an expression of win/lose metrics) and not for resiliency and life.

2. The second generator function is **the deconstruction of intrinsic value** itself. The deconstruction of value is the sense that human value does not participate in the intrinsic value of the Real, for the Real is dogmatically declared to have no intrinsic value. Thus, there is no shared identity between the interior of the human being and Reality. There is no common participation in a field of shared intrinsic value. Instead of being intimate with value, we are alienated from value. And only intrinsic value can arouse will: political, moral, and social will.

To sum up, without a shared grammar of value there is no global intimacy, and therefore no global coherence, and no global coordination in response to catastrophic and existential risk, which means, put simply, there will be, quite literally, no future.

HEALING THE GLOBAL INTIMACY DISORDER REQUIRES THE EVOLUTION OF INTIMACY

But we are not hopeless. On the contrary, we are filled with great hope. Hope is a memory of the future. That memory of the future *is* the direct hit that takes down the Death Star, the culture of death. **The direct hit must be**—as it has always been in history—**the emergence of a new stage of evolution**.

Crisis is an evolutionary driver, and every crisis is, at its core, a crisis of intimacy: from the oxygen crisis of the single cells dying which generated multicellular life at the dawn of existence, to the existential risk in this very moment.[9]

The direct hit is therefore structurally self-evident: the evolution of intimacy itself.

What is intimacy, as a structure of Cosmos all the way down and all the way up the evolutionary chain? We engage this inquiry in depth in other writings, but for now we will simply adduce what we have called the "Intimacy Equation":

> *Intimacy = shared identity in the context of [relative] otherness* × *mutuality of recognition* × *mutuality of pathos* × *mutuality of value* × *mutuality of purpose*

Intimacy is about the capacity of parts to generate a *shared identity* while retaining their otherness, or distinct identity. This requires multiple mutualities, including recognition, pathos (or feeling), value, and purpose. The parts must recognize and feel each other, even as they share value and purpose. But all of this must lead to intimate union—and not pathological

---

9 We demonstrate this principle in some depth in the multi-volume series, *The Universe: A Love Story* (forthcoming) (https://worldphilosophyandreligion.org/early-ontologies), *The Intimate Universe: Global Intimacy Disorder as Cause for Global Action Paralysis* (forthcoming), and in other writings of CosmoErotic Humanism.

fusion, where the distinct identity of the parts disappears—like subatomic particles that successfully become an atom, or two people who successfully become a couple.

THE DECONSTRUCTION OF VALUE IS THE DECONSTRUCTION OF INTIMACY

We have identified the global intimacy disorder as the root cause of existential risk. But the underlying ultimate failure of intimacy is the deconstruction of value itself.

The deconstruction of value means that human value does not participate in any sense of intrinsic value of the Real. This is not about individual *values,* but about *the Field of Value* that underlies all of them. **When the human being**—moved, often sincerely or even nobly, by myriad cultural, historical, and psychological confusions—**claims to have stepped out of the Field of Value, then intimacy itself is deconstructed.**

The deconstruction of value is the deconstruction of intimacy.

In the absence of a shared Story of Value, a story that is an authentic expression of Reality's Eros, a story rooted in *pseudo-Eros* takes center stage and becomes the generator function for existential risk. Our modern pseudo-Eros story is *rivalrous conflict governed by win/lose metrics.* Such a story catalyzes in its wake the second generator function of existential risk: *complicated fragile systems with no allurement or intimacy between the parts.* It is in that sense that we have argued that the first generator function for existential risk is the success story.

- The failure of intimacy is precisely the impotent experience that there is no shared identity between the interior of the human being and Reality. **There is no shared identity in the sense of any kind of common participation in a field of shared intrinsic value.**
- **But only a shared Story of Value can arouse the global will**

required to engage catastrophic and existential risk. For it is only global political, moral, and social will—and we can even say *erotic* will—that can generate the most Good, True and Beautiful world that we have always known is possible.

THE EVOLUTION OF LOVE IS THE TELLING OF A NEW STORY

Coupled with the Intimacy Equation is the scientifically grounded realization, in both the exterior and interior sciences, that Reality is a progressive deepening of intimacies, or, said slightly differently:

Reality is Evolution. Evolution is the evolution of intimacy.

- ◆ The evolution of intimacy requires—both personally and collectively—a deeper, more accurate discernment of the nature of our universe, ourselves, and our beloveds.
- ◆ This new discernment generates a new global Story of Value.
- ◆ The new global Story of Value generates an emergent, heretofore unseen global intimacy and heals the global intimacy disorder.

The new Story of Value is the direct hit that takes down the Death Star and replaces it with the hope that invokes the memory of our best future.

Global intimacy facilitates global coherence, which facilitates global coordination, which activates the possibility of our creative and effectively coordinated global responses to the global meta-crisis in its entirety and its specific expressions.

To solve Bertrand Russell's challenge—the apparent argument for the subjectivity of ethical values—**we have to reground value theory in eternal yet evolving First Principles and First Values, and articulate a new Story of Value.**

This is what we call CosmoErotic Humanism.

CosmoErotic Humanism—together with other emergent strands—**needs to become the ground of a world religion as a context for our diversity**. We need religion, even as we need science, to articulate a shared global grammar of value.

As we said at the beginning, our choice is simple: love or die.

- To love means to participate in the evolution of love, which is the evolution of the human Story of Value.
- To love means to evolve and activate a new cultural enlightenment—rooted in a new narrative of identity, a new narrative of value, a new narrative of intimate communion, a new narrative of desire, a new narrative of power—all of which will birth new narratives of economics and politics.
- The evolution of love is the telling of a new Story.

The new Story that must be told is a love story, for in fact that is the deepest truth of Reality, rooted in the best exterior and interior sciences, that we have at this moment in time:

- Reality is not merely a fact. Reality is a story.
- Reality is not an ordinary story. Reality is a love story.
- Reality is not an ordinary love story. Reality is an Outrageous Love Story.

Story doesn't mean it's *made-up*.

It means doing the hard work of integrating the validated insights of the traditional world, the modern world, and the postmodern world.

This is the intention at the heart of telling the new Story of CosmoErotic Humanism.

ABOUT THIS VOLUME

We live in a time of crisis, what CosmoErotic Humanism[1] refers to as "a time between worlds and a time between stories." To respond, we need to evolve. Only profound evolution—transformation—will tip the scale away from its natural trajectory of catastrophic devolution.

First and foremost, we need the right diagnosis of the crisis. For many years, Barbara located the core of the crisis in the narrative arc of culture—the "success story." The success story has one plotline: rivalrous conflict governed by win/loss metrics.

Barbara and Marc together deepened this diagnosis, locating the crisis in a deeper root structure that underlies the success story—what Marc has long referred to as a "global intimacy disorder." Barbara and Marc came to the profound understanding—rooted in extensive analysis of both interior (subjective experience) and exterior (classic sciences) data sets—that the core driver of the current crisis is no less than a crisis of intimacy.

The reader is invited on a journey to understand how transformation, power, and intimacy are interwoven strands of the fundamental fabric of Cosmos.

Emergent from this set of realizations, we understand that evolution itself is a series of transformations activated and actualized through ever deepening intimacies. In other words, evolution is the progressive deepening of intimacies.

Moreover, not only do we live in the Intimate Universe, but the Intimate Universe also lives in us. As such, we have the capacity to participate in

---

1 For a deeper dive, see David J. Temple, *First Principles and First Values: Forty-two Propositions on CosmoErotic Humanism* (2024).

evolution through the personal transformation of our own intimacies. Therefore, the core realization of the new human is that my transformation is the transformation of the whole.

The deepening of intimacy is the invitation and demand of our time. The ultimate human dignity is the realization that we are—each of us— unique configurations of intimacy. As we have articulated in CosmoErotic Humanism, the new name of God is the Infinite Intimate. We are God's unique intimacies.

As such, each of us is intended, recognized, desired, acknowledged, chosen, loved, adored, and needed by all of Reality—so that we enact this transformation through deepening intimacy.

Our crisis is a birth. But for the crisis of intimacy to become a birth, intimacy itself must deepen, intensify, and widen its circle. Everyone, every part of ourselves, and all of the othered beings who have been placed outside must be welcomed back into our circle of intimacy.

Intimacy is intimately bound up with desire. Indeed, intimacy itself is our core desire. When we clarify our interior, we access our deepest heart's desire. We make contact with the desire to go all the way in this lifetime, to become intimate with all of ourselves, with all of our beloved, with all of our beloveds, and ultimately, with All-That-Is as our Beloved. We embrace the blaze of light in every word, our holy and broken *Hallelujahs*. We need to be madly in love with ourselves, which is, of course, from a clinical and covenantal perspective, precisely the opposite of narcissism.

Intimacy, however, is not generic. Intimacy is always unique. We need to claim our identity as irreducible Unique Selves, higher individuations beyond ego, unique discretions of True Self. We are unique incarnations of the LoveIntelligence and LoveBeauty of All-That-Is, living in us, as us, and through us.

Moreover, we need to become intimate with our Unique Selves. For the essence of the new human—their creative and transformative power— derives only from the deepest depth of intimacy with their own self.

We need to become intimate with our own power. So much of our power has been split off and exiled outside the circle. We must leave behind the tired old demonization of power and realize that clarified power is a direct expression of clarified love.

Our power lies in the radically unique personal transformation that is ours to do. When we truly embody the realization that our unique personal transformation transforms the whole, we experience the most profound pleasure possible: the pleasure of clarified power in devotion to the Beloved—the Beloved of Reality herself.

- We need to become intimate with the clarified sacred texts of culture of all the epochs of human history.
- We need to ground our evolving culture on profound intimacy with the present, which collects the memories of the past and hopes for the memories of the future.
- We need to be intimate with past, present, and future—and that intimate knowing is the ground of our interior sciences.

We are the ones to enact the healing of the intimacy crisis. This is our greatest desire and greatest power and greatest pleasure: to be intimacy and thus to be transformation—to know that your personal transformation, with right evolutionary intention, participates literally and ontologically in the transformation of the whole thing.

The emergence of somatic, sensual, and scientific gnosis is what we call the journey from *Homo armor* to *Homo amor*. It marks the emergence of the new human and the new humanity. The temple of intimacy is built when we stay in and go all the way in this lifetime.

Volume 11

These oral essays are edited talks delivered by Marc Gafni and Barbara Marx Hubbard between September and November 2018.

CHAPTER ONE

TRANSFORMATION HAPPENS AT THE EDGE

Episode 101 — September 22, 2018

EVOLUTIONARY LOVE CODE: I AM A UNIQUE CONFIGURATION OF DESIRE

The Field of Intimacy and Desire is seamless but not featureless.

I am a unique feature of the larger Field of Intimacy and Desire.

I am a unique configuration of desire and intimacy.

I CANNOT BE INTIMATE WITHOUT YOU

As we incorporate this code, we realize we are God in expression, now this very second. We are the process of creation which desires intimacy as us. Our intimacy is a unique configuration of desire and Eros, with God intending us all uniquely—everyone simultaneously on planet Earth as one of the many billions of planets in the universe.

This is a moment that is both nascent—it's just being born—even as it's triumphant. It's triumphant because we have established the church. The establishment of the church is just the very beginning.

1

What is the goal of Evolutionary Church? The goal is to love each other open. The goal is bigger than serving every one of us. There is a core sentence in church: *I am not willing to be written in the Book of Life without you.*

That is a new dimension. It's about the Unique Self Symphony. That's the understanding. As in the code, we are part of a larger Field of Intimacy. Because I am part of a larger Field of Intimacy and a larger Field of Desire, then my unique expression of desire and intimacy cannot actually desire and cannot be intimate *without you.*

We have to come together in a new configuration of intimacy. Evolution itself is the evolution of intimacy. Whenever we have a crisis, our crisis is a birth. Our crisis of intimacy is a birth. The desire is for more intimacy, but not just more intimacy. It's the desire that drives evolution, as we say in Evolutionary Church. One of our codes is: **Evolution is the progressive deepening of intimacies.** It doesn't just deepen; it deepens through new configurations.

At this moment in time, in every moment of time, the precise new configuration of intimacy available to meet the crisis is the new map. This is codified in what we call the Wheel of Co-Creation 2.0. A new code is to codify. **We codify so that we can actually download it into the source code of culture.**

SYMPHONY MEANS FEELING THE FIELD

What is the new configuration of intimacy that addresses the crisis of this moment, as we are going through a phase shift, which is occurring after a very long period of time? It hasn't happened for thousands of years. There's a phase shift where:

- Governance is shifting.
- Infrastructure is shifting.
- Identity is shifting.
- Relationships are shifting.

The entire multilayered infrastructure of Reality is shifting before our eyes. It's shifting at an exponential speed. When that happens, in order for us to receive and facilitate the shift, for it to become a birth and not an utter breakdown, we need a new source code.

When we say utter breakdown, let's understand what that means: that which causes untold death, pain, and suffering to the most vulnerable among us. That is what it means.

Let's take this out of words and imagine:

You can't eat—for two hours you can't eat anything. Now imagine you can't eat for a day. All right, now for two days. Imagine what that feels like. Just imagine in your body and then exponentialize that feeling of pain and discomfort for three days, and four, and five days.

Your children can't eat and now the water is flooding your house. Now you are stranded.

We are talking about a very real thing. This is not abstract. A very real, massive amount of suffering for the most dislocated and vulnerable among us as the various existential risks play themselves out—unless we enact a new vision of intimacy. That's what we are talking about.

This is about healing suffering, but it's healing suffering by opening a *soup kitchen of memetic codes*. That's what we're doing in church. This is a universal, galactic soup kitchen. And in this soup kitchen, we're feeding not just soup for the next meal, but the very soup of Reality in the very source code of Reality.

So, when we say, *I'm not willing to be written in the Book of Life without you*, we're invoking something new which relates to this week's code, which is Unique Self Symphony. You learn to symphonize. It's very hard to do. It's not easy, and a person can say all the right words but can't symphonize.

Symphony means I hear the resonant music. I feel the field. But not just abstractly. When I feel the field, I feel the three people next to me. Let's start there. I feel the field right around me, then I feel a larger field of how my actions impact the larger field, or don't impact the larger field. Then I feel the field is even wider. It's more worldcentric and broader.

That's what I means when I say, *I'm not willing to be written in the Book of Life without you.* That refers to two aspects. First, the identity code is that *I'm a unique configuration of desire and intimacy.* Then the larger code, the field code, is that the Field of Intimacy and Desire is seamless, but not featureless.

Evolutionary Church is a re-coding project. We are re-coding. The Field of Intimacy and Desire is seamless but not featureless.

- The field is *seamless.*
- The field is *not featureless,* meaning, it's not just *the One.* It's not just featureless.
- It has unique features, and who are its unique features? You and me!
- I'm a unique feature of the larger Field of Intimacy and Desire.
- I'm a unique configuration of desire and intimacy that's part of this larger field which is itself now generating a new structure of intimacy.

That new structure of intimacy is Unique Self Symphony. In Evolutionary Church, this expresses itself in our commitment to reach a million people, and seven million people. We have to find the people all over the world who are going to join us. We're pouring ourselves into the church so we can affect the field all over the world.

But what is the goal of that? Why are we doing that? Here is our word: *A Planetary Awakening in Love through Unique Self Symphony.* That's the whole story and we can never lose sight of that. That's what we are here for. Our Evolutionary Church is dedicated to madly loving each other open. We"re a band of Evolutionary Lovers, Outrageous Lovers, loving the moment open in every second.

But not just a moment—that moment is in evolutionary time. This moment is in an evolutionary context—I realize who I am: I'm a unique configuration of intimacy and desire, and to love you means I love your unique configuration of intimacy and desire.

I love you so much. I love your unique configuration of intimacy and desire.

Do you get that I love that?

That's gorgeous and beautiful, and our configurations come together in a Unique Self Symphony.

THE RITUAL OF PRAYER UNITES US IN THE FIELD

Now, in order to do that, and to feel that, and to be that, we have to pray. What does it mean to pray? When we pray we don't pray to the god who doesn't exist. The god you don't believe in doesn't exist. **When we pray, we bring it to the Field of Intimacy and Desire, which is God.** God is the Infinity of Intimacy, not just the Infinity of Power. That's another one of our codes.

And so, I come to the Infinity of Intimacy. I come to the field, the Force that holds me, and I say, *Oh, my god, can I just tell you something?* Being a unique configuration of intimacy and desire, I mean, sometimes it's so triumphant and sometimes it's just wracked with pain. Sometimes it hurts so much.

- We see through the eye of our wounds.
- Our wound is the aperture through which we see.
- Our wound is our *holy and our broken Hallelujah.*
- We don't leave our wounds behind, and we don't leave our triumphs behind.
- We bring all of it into the field.
- That's what prayer means.

We're going to walk into the field together. We're going to step out of our particular place in the field, and step into the wider field to offer into the field our holy and our broken *Hallelujah*.

The very second we do that, we realize we're not alone.

The field is awake—it's intelligent, it's alive.

As we have said in the pointing out instructions for prayer: *If I can hear a friend talking, of course, the Field can hear the friend talking.* That's what prayer means: of course, the Field can hear me.

We've lost something in the Human Potential and New Age movement. **In all the New Age movements we've lost the power of ritual, and the power of doing something with depth and intention repetitively which creates a field of morphic resonance.**

Paradoxically, the fundamentalist world is better than us at that. In order to effect transformation, to create a field, the gorgeous civil rights movement in America could not have made it without the Gospel Church in America, and all its rituals.

The new Gospel Church is Evolutionary Church. And even though there's a sad and sordid history of churches, we're liberating the spark of the holy and creating a *post-church church*, a post-dogmatic church. We resonate together in ritual, even as everyone prays in the way they want.

But the point is that we can step into the field, together and we offer prayer just by opening with the same words, *I pray*, which then unites us in the field. We step out of our hyper-individuality, and we begin to feel the symphony. So, while anyone can pray in whatever way they want, let's also create shared base of music in the symphony, a shared base of practice.

That is part of what we're trying to reclaim in church. **We're reclaiming the higher vision of God, the higher vision of church, which is absolutely critical.**

WE CELEBRATE THE EVOLUTION OF CULTURE IN ALL FIELDS

I want to point out something truly exciting about *being* the evolution of intimacy and desire. We've been talking about humanity at the shift point between devolution, terrible destruction and pain, on one hand, and the evolution of love, creativity, potentiality, that could take us to the other side of the shift.

I want to take a moment to declare, reveal, and discover how it's happening in every cultural aspect of our lives. It's very, very hard to see because it's not the news. The news is about everything that isn't working. **The *new* news is about everything that's emerging.**

The church itself, as it was in the early church, is the place where we gather for the entire *dharma* to come through. I (Barbara) was just reviewing briefly how that *dharma* has come through me. I decided, for example, to bring the *dharma* into politics. Without any possibility of being vice president of the United States, I decided to run to be selected as the vice president. This enabled me to make a speech for us all to say that the new politics is activating, connecting, and expressing what's working, and new, and emerging in the world.

Now, let's take science. For the scientific community, we're writing *The Universe: A Love Story*, by taking all the scientific and psychological truths and integrating them into a formation of the love story of this new humanity. Let's bring science in there.

Our friends at the Intergalactic University have demonstrated the reality of contact with life beyond this planet hundreds and hundreds, if not thousands and thousands of times, but which is not yet recognized by science.

Here we're saying: Okay, science is going to have to expand to include itself in this reality.

Then let's take, well, spirituality itself. What we're doing here is we're evolving spirituality very much the way Jesus did. When he said, *if you have seen me, you have seen Reality. If you see me, I am you, and you are me.*

We are saying—along with Jesus, the Buddha, and every great religious leader—that we are that.

We're showing up in science.

We're showing up in politics.

We're showing up in religion.

We're showing up in the media.

We're now planting the seed of this emerging Reality in every discipline of society.

In the Evolutionary Church, **I invite us to see ourselves as *post*-shift, planting a place where everyone who is shifting knows they can go.**

- We're not shifting into a vacuum.
- We're not shifting into a space with nobody in it;
- We're shifting into a space where all the new humans are congregating.
- We're shifting into a space where the desire of God for greater intimacy, for Eros, is happening through our joining.

If you're going to do the new science, the new politics, the new spirituality, you have to join intimately with each other. You have to join intimately so that you overcome the illusion of separateness that keeps all these divisions separate from each other, including all the religions in the world.

We're overcoming all those divisions by the desire in each of us for intimacy with the Divine, with each other, and with the clusters of people now populating the social scene with the new humanity.

I believe that in the same short period that we could go down into devolution and destruction, we can create the new fields in every relationship of culture as depicted in the Wheel of Co-Creation, including justice, science, government, and relationships.

All of them are being populated by exactly this desire, and this intimacy, and this inner knowing that the Book of Life will not be written without each other. Let us have a collective prayer in this moment for the culture of humanity, knowing that the desire of God is for greater intimacy in every field, and that this intimacy is now being realized.

We can celebrate the evolution of culture itself in all these fields, with all these people now stepping into the future as the desire of God for greater intimacy, connectivity, and love.

ONE HUNDRED AND ONE IS THE PATHWAY TO THE OTHER SIDE

The present desire of God for intimacy right now is the memory of the future.

We're creating, all of us together, this gorgeous new emergent, because intimacy generates emergence.

- ♦ How do we do it?
- ♦ How do we get to the other side?
- ♦ What does it mean to be on the other side?

Here is the pathway to the other side.

There's only one path to the other side. You can't declare it; you can't affirm it.

There's one path and one path only to the other side. It's the path of 101.

9

I want to share with you a secret, a beautiful text from the third century and have it emerge now in the twenty-first century and show us the path to the other side. The text reads as follows:

> *One who studies a hundred times doesn't worship God, but one who studies a hundred and one times is one who worships God.*

What does that mean? What does that mean when you study at 101? We are in week one hundred and one, and last week, we were at a 100. We have this hidden evolutionary text that says anyone who studies a hundred times hasn't served God.

They haven't served evolution.

They haven't served the evolutionary impulse.

They haven't served Outrageous Love.

When you do 101, that's when you begin to step to the other side. It's through 101 that you get to the other side. You begin to serve and awaken as the evolutionary impulse. Why is that?

Do you remember being in the gym? Let's say you are weightlifting in the gym. When you do weightlifting, you do let's say three sets, each with ten reps. You do ten reps on each set. So, how does it work, your first set of ten reps? If you're really strong, you lift pretty easily. It's great. Then you go to your second set of reps. Okay, now you have done your second set of 10 reps. A bit more slowly, but you're still feeling pretty good.

Now you're in your third set of ten reps. Now you're at the end, right? You are like, *oh my God*, on the eighth rep, and then it's the ninth. All right, you are trying to push it up and it's like, *oh, my God!* You're trying to push up the tenth, and it's like *ahhh*, and you finally get up the tenth.

That's where growth happens. That's where transformation happens.

Transformation happens at the very edge.

It's that place where I push myself. It's a place where I make an internal, loving, mad, outrageous, love demand, that I show up more than I have ever shown up; that I reach more than I've ever reached. I go deep inside of me, and I go deep inside me in the place that's hard.

I go to the place that's uncomfortable. I don't quite feel well. I'm not quite on. I'm feeling a little uncomfortable, and I'm feeling challenged. Maybe I'm angry or maybe I'm hurt.

It's when it doesn't feel perfect to me that I reach inside, and *I find who I am.* I recognize my identity: I am an Outrageous Lover. I am a unique configuration of intimacy and desire in a larger Field of Desire. I cannot be written in the Book of Life without you.

- When I reach inside at the moment that's hard.
- When I *mythologize* the other human being before me instead of *pathologizing.*
- When I confess, not only *my* greatness, but I confess *your* greatness.
- When I'm a lover who sees with God's eyes at the moments when I'm broken and my heart is devastated.
- When I hold the field and the impact of my actions. I don't go blind because I'm so excited or lost in some dimension of myself.
- It's when I step out of myself to find my highest self.
- When I lose my ego to find my Unique Self.
- When I lose my contraction to find my expansion.
- When I become spontaneous, extemporaneous, contemporaneous, with you. We are doing it together.

It's at that moment of struggle. You can't get to the other side without saying that, *in the moment when it's hard, when I could break down, instead I'm going to break through.* **At that moment of emergency, I emerge.**

11

That is how you get to the other side. You commit that in a time of breakdown, you're going to break through. Every single one of us in this church has had times of breakdown. We have had times of emergency. We've had times when we feel despair, but we go into the despair, and we *turn fate into destiny.*

When we are in breakdown, we recognize our deepest identity:

- I am a unique configuration of intimacy and desire.
- I am needed by All-That-Is, I am chosen, I am adored, I am intended, I am loved. I have a song to sing and a poem to write that can't be lived, or written, or breathed, by anyone that ever was, is, will be, other than me.

It's when and only when I do that, that I have the right to declare, *I am on the other side.*

It is with a commitment to 101. One hundred is not enough. At one hundred, I'm just doing my thing, but at 101—meaning that I am willing to push to the other side no matter what it takes, no matter when it is—I'm breaking through.

When I'm in despair, when I'm broken down, I'm going to break through.

When I fall, I'm going to get up.

When I cry, I'm going to turn those tears into laughter.

I'm always going to turn it around.

I'm always going to turn fate into destiny.

I may fall a thousand times, but I'm going to get up stronger each time again, like a lion from the fire.

The temple of intimacy is built when we stay in.

12

The other side doesn't mean we are perfected. We are all holy and broken *Hallelujahs*. We are all imperfect vessels for the light, but we're on the other side. We are committed to turning fate into destiny.

I want to just invite you to one more thing. Sometimes, we walk a big path with someone and then we leave them behind, and we always have to let people go for it.

Whenever you give someone a ring of commitment, you're always saying, *with this ring, I set you free*. Here's the other side of that statement: When we can remain together and walk together, even as the configurations of intimacy change, we build a temple. We can find a way to heal the wounds. **The temple is built when we rebuild after the wounds and after the crisis**.

Christianity is built on a madly loving response to breakdown. Find someone in your life who you were walking with and for some reason you stopped walking. It might have been completely right. Maybe you got divorced. Maybe someone passed away and you forgot about them, except they're on the other side, and you can't find them.

Find people who were in your life and if you can, come back together with them, maybe it will be in prayer. Maybe it will be an action. Let's find the people we've left behind—each one of us—because it was just too hard and goes too deep in our hearts. And let's take them with us to the other side.

CHAPTER TWO

BEYOND MASLOW: EVOLUTIONARY PRAYER AND THE SIX CORE HUMAN NEEDS

Episode 102 — September 29, 2018

EVOLUTIONARY LOVE CODE: I AM A UNIQUE FEATURE OF THE FIELD OF INTIMACY

The Field of Intimacy and Desire is seamless, but it is not featureless.

I am a unique feature of the Field of Intimacy and Desire.

I am a unique configuration of desire and intimacy.

WE RESONATE AND RECAPITULATE TO EVOLVE THE SOURCE CODE

This is an opening of our own intimacy and desire. Nature creates intimacy for ever more desire to be realized.

Let's put our attention on our deepest heart's desire, and on the intimacies that will fulfill that desire. What expression of that unique configuration of desire would be fulfilled in the deepest intimacy that is open for you?

There, at that exact point of desire and intimacy joining, you have the new humanity, the new human, the new future, the world at the next stage of evolution. Consider a world in which that unique configuration of people's desire and intimacy is cultivated. What kind of world is at the threshold here?

Often, we recapitulate from week to week. **The process of doing a recapitulation is to use the exact, right words that we used in the *dharma* and then to order the points clearly again.** Once you do that, once you take that in, at that level of fully receiving it, then you can create with it. Before we translate the *dharma* into a different language receive it in its own language. Its own language is resonant. It 's a kind of sacred text. When you can feel its very specific language, then it becomes alive. Then it becomes vibrant. Then it begins to transform. There is this step. Before we *place it in a different bucket of knowledge*, let's be in it directly.

One of our good friends is very involved in the codes of the Pentagon. He said that one of the big problems today is that there's so much noise. There's so much noise that it's very hard for the authentic codes, as it were, to be discerned. We were able to trace things earlier in the virtual world, twenty-five years ago, because there was very little there. Now there's such a plethora of information that it's very hard to discern information from wisdom. So, it's really important that we're trying to evolve the source code here.

When I am talking to you now, I am speaking to *you*. You are speaking to me. We are speaking together. We are also speaking to the future. We are not just determined by our past. We are not just pandering to the present.

- ◆ We are prophesying the future.
- ◆ We are anticipating the future.
- ◆ We are creating a memory of the future, in the present.

We are doing it by trying to understand the deepest structure of Reality itself and what it demands of us, what it invites us to. That is what the *dharma* is.

We resonate the codes. **Resonance is a musical term.**

---

*Resonance means I am feeling
the inside of it and opening it.
We are opening the code.*

We're setting it up in context. We are beginning the process. Without resonance, we can't enter. From resonance we move to prayer.

We recapitulate so that it doesn't become automatic, so that we notice what's happening. Now we are moving into prayer. Prayer is gorgeous! The evolution of prayer and the evolution of God is one of the core commitments of Evolutionary Church.

THE LARGER FIELD OF INTELLIGENCE CAN HEAR ME TALKING

As we step into prayer, I want to walk you through our three core meditations, because I really want to get them with you in a very precise order, so we will really have them. I want to go back to the original symphony, as it were, that we've done over the last couple of years, so we can feel how the pieces flow.

It starts with a simple *pointing out*. The first piece is called a *pointing-out instruction*, a term I borrowed from the Tibetan Buddhists. The *pointing out* is simple. It goes something like this:

Marc: Barbara, did you hear me talking?

Barbara: Of course I heard you talking, Marc. What are you asking me that for? That's a dumb question. You don't think I was listening?

Marc: But Barbara, what part of you heard me?

Barbara: My ears.

Marc: It couldn't be just your ears because ears are just technical structures.

Barbara: Well, it wasn't just my ears. It was my consciousness, my intelligence.

Marc: Well, beloved Barbara, I know you are wildly conscious and intelligent; after all, you're Barbara Marx Hubbard! But are you the most conscious and intelligent person in all of the United States?

Barbara: Well, there might be someone in Idaho. You know what I mean? Some place, somewhere. In other words, we all know that there's somebody.

Marc: Is your consciousness and intelligence, which heard me talking, cut off from the larger Field of Consciousness and Intelligence?

Barbara: Of course not! I actually feel that my consciousness and intelligence is part of a larger field.

Marc: Beloved, if you can hear me talking, and it's your consciousness and intelligence that hears me talking, is it possible that the entire Field of Consciousness and Intelligence can't hear me talking?

Barbara: Of course not!

That's the pointing-out instruction. It's gorgeous!

Why is it gorgeous? What a pointing-out instruction does it that cuts through all the theology. It cuts through all the two thousand years' worth of books written on this, and I have read too many of them. It's one simple pointing-out instruction. It cuts through. It allows you to find your own enlightened truth that already lives in you.

Barbara knows that it's not just her technical ears that hear, it's *Barbara-ness* hearing, which is consciousness and intelligence. That *Barbara-ness* is not cut off from the larger field, and then all of a sudden, I realize, oh my God, *Barbara can hear me talking, her consciousness and intelligence. Of course, the larger Field of Intelligence can hear me talking.*

That's what we mean when we say,:

Prayers are heard. Oh, my Goddess! That's shocking!

The entire New Age, Human Potential world doesn't get this, which means that you lose your connection to the Divinity that hears your voice. Do you understand how tragic that is?

Instead, there comes a kind of myopic, egoic, grandstanding and commodifying of Spirit because there's no larger Spirit actually hearing me. So, now we're going to fight for *market share* and *lists*. There's no larger conversation.

When we get the essence of prayer, it changes who we are. That's the first step. Then we go a second step.

EVOLUTIONARY MEDITATIONS FOR PRAYING TO GOD IN THE FIRST, SECOND, AND THIRD PERSON

Now, we move from a pointing-out instruction to meditation. In the meditation, we do something really simple. We shut our eyes, and we say, *Imagine God in the third person.* Versions of *God in the third person*, that technical term, appear in many texts.

In the *Zohar* we talk about God as first, second, and third.

- *Ani*, God is "I," in the first person.
- *Atah*, God is you, in the second person.
- *Hu*, God in the third person.

God in third person is the God who is the intelligence of Cosmos. It's all the mathematical formulas exponentialized that Albert Einstein, in 1914, used to develop the theory of relativity.

- It's all the laws of physics, all the laws of chemistry.
- It's all of geology. It is all of biology.
- It's all of neuroscience. It's the millions of miles of nerve cable that are in your body. It's the fifty trillion cells.
- It's the emotional, existential, physical complementarity, unlike any that ever was.
- It's the entire system within systems within systems, not only of you, and your immediate environment. We actually extend out into the galaxy. Then we extend out into a hundred billion galaxies. Then we move into multiverses.

And all of that is the third person. **God in the third person is the force, the energy, the power of divinity**. The Infinity of Energy. The Infinity of Intelligence. The Infinity of Power. The Infinity of dazzling complexity. The Infinity of Brilliance that all the supercomputers in the world exponentialized couldn't access.

Then, in this meditation, you take all of that, and place it in a chair next to you, at this very moment. All of that is sitting in a chair, incarnate, in a body, looking at you and loving you madly.

That's God in the second person. That is called, in Christianity, the mystery of Incarnation. Isn't that gorgeous? It is stunning!

That's the mystery of Incarnation. That is what it means.

Then we ask a question: What does that Christ figure—that God figure, that incarnated figure sitting in a chair—feel like when He/She/It looks at you? What does He/She/It feel like?

To discover that, we continue this meditation by saying, *now access your most tender moment.* So tender, your most tender moment:

- You're looking at your child.
- You're looking at a Beloved.
- You're looking at a sister, a brother.
- You're feeling so tender, and so loving, so wanting to care, and so wanting to nurture.
- You're willing to lay everything down for that person.

Imagine that feeling and now double it. Triple it. Quadruple it. Times ten. Times a hundred. Times a thousand. Times a hundred thousand. Times a million. Times a billion times, exponentialized: **quivering tenderness, all the way into infinity.**

Now hold that. Let's access another feeling of God in second person. In our third meditation, move over and access the experience of desire. Raw desire rising in you, at some point when it may have happened in your life. Or, if it has never happened to you, imagine desire.

Your most intense, raw desire for a person, an idea, food. Raw desire. Now double it. Triple it. Quadruple it. Times ten. Times a hundred. Times a thousand. Times a hundred thousand. A million. A billion.

Desire exponentialized, quivering into infinity.

Now take those two, *quivering-into-infinity-tenderness* and *quivering-into-infinity-desire*, and hold them, one in each hand. Take your hands, as balls of fire, and bring them together as one.

Put them inside the heart of that figure in the chair, looking at you.

That's what that figure in that chair, He/She/It, feels for you: infinite, nourishing, tender, quivering care and complete, absolute, radical desire for you.

Any part of you that just accessed any piece of that, right now, the part that understood—that part is *already awake.* That's the enlightenment of God in the second person. That's what we mean when we say, before prayer, that God is not only the Infinity of Power—that God is not only *tat tvam asi,* Thou Art That, the Divine that resides as you, in you.

God is also the Infinity of Intimacy that knows your name, that cares for you and desires you intimately in every detail, in every gesture, in every gesticulation, in every flourish of your life, internally and externally. To know that is to be held, is to be awake. It is the *knowing* that changes everything. It is the knowing of the Infinity of Intimacy that we bring into prayer.

We pray before that Infinity of Intimacy, on the altar of the Infinity of Intimacy, that we sometimes call God. The god you don't believe in doesn't exist. God is the Infinity of Intimacy, to whom we bring everything.

The Infinity of Intimacy is our boyfriend, our girlfriend, our lover, our beloved.

The Infinity of Intimacy is our Outrageous Lover, our Evolutionary Lover who says, *Bring me everything. Don't leave anything out. If you feel hurt, bring me everything. Bring all of your holy and broken Hallelujah to me.*

Let's do that right now, for the sake of all Cosmos, for the sake of the evolution of love. For the sake of each one of us here in church. For the sake of the growth of this church exponentialized, to become a force for healing and transformation. For evolutionary unfolding.

The evolutionary impulse is incarnate as this church, in this church, through this church. We bring our holy and our broken *Hallelujah* before the altar of the Infinity of Intimacy in this present moment of the eternal and evolving Now.

REALIZING *I AM GOD IN EVOLUTION* AT THE JUMP POINT

It starts out with the phrase, *I am God in evolution.* I want to take this literally. We, you, all of us are that entire force of creation. Both the personal experience of each of us as well as the genius that it took to go the 13.7 billion years to me and you now, at the very crossroads of evolution, where the system could go into devolution, or it could rise to the next stage of evolution.

What I mean is that every single individual is on that shift point of this punctuated equilibrium. Evolution is concerned more with purpose than with species. The purpose of each of us now, in this Evolutionary Church is to realize that *I am God in evolution. I am an expression of the uniqueness of who I am, as God in evolution, now creating a contribution.* **Every one of us creating is absolutely required to contribute to the whole system at the point of devolution or evolution.**

We are giving thanks for living at the exact moment in history where each person, as God in evolution, can affect the direction of the whole system, because each of us is intrinsic to the intimacy of the system that we are part of. Just as every cell in our body can affect the whole body, every cell in the planetary body can affect the whole body.

Every person in the Evolutionary Church, as a unique expression of divine creativity, is coming together—like nature does—into synergistic convergence, both on the inner plane of love, Spirit, and prayer, and then on the outer plane of co-creative action.

I'm beginning to see this church of Evolutionary Love as an expression of (probably the first to arise on this Earth from what I am aware of) what it truly is like to be a cluster of humans who believe *I am God in evolution. I am the intention of creation. I am the intimacy of desire of the greater process of evolution.*

Those people, coming together in synergistic convergence and the realization of our desires through prayer, co-creation, and other ways of us joining together, are just at the beginning of the most awesome contribution to the evolution of the world, right now. I really see that.

At every one of these shift points of evolution, when it could have gone into greater devolution and where so many species became extinct, there was always a species somewhere that connected enough separate parts to take a jump: from single cell to multi-cell, from to animal to human.

Now we are the jump point. The joining of genius through unique vocational arousal of each of us, unique and brilliant as we are, can make the jump. As more of us come in, imagine the effect that this congregation of evolutionary impulse, genius, desire, and intimacy could have on the evolutionary shift point that we are in now.

Imagine, as in the early church when a few people got together who believed Jesus, and believed in the Second Coming of Christ so much so that they were willing to go into lions' dens. They were willing to die for this, willing to give their life for this.

If we are as great as that, believing in the Second Coming of humanity, believing in each of us as an expression of the impulse of creation, incarnate as you and me, joined in a cluster of shared purpose, what might be possible? While nature cares for species, nature also preserves purpose, regardless of which species survive.

The enormous purpose of the Church of Evolutionary Love (a critical expression at this shift point of evolution), is that when evolution can go in whatever direction, we are the ones making up evolution, right now. That is what all this means.

I'm imagining the entire Evolutionary Church, from all over the world, as it grows, being critical to the shift point of evolution, being the activator, being the inspiration of us coming together as a whole species, capable of healing the Earth.

I'm imagining us capable of freeing ourselves from hunger, disease, and war, alleviating suffering such that we can penetrate into a universe of billions of other galaxies and planets, many of which, it's said, have life comparable to our own. This is the moment.

BEYOND MASLOW: THE VISION OF SIX CORE HUMAN NEEDS THAT CHANGES EVERYTHING

Let's look at our code again:

> The Field of Intimacy and Desire is seamless, but it is not featureless. I am a unique feature of the larger Field of Intimacy and Desire.

If I get that, my whole life changes. Just that sentence.

I am a unique feature of the larger Field of Intimacy and Desire, meaning there is no local intimacy. I can't try to be intimate with my close friend, or even with my evolutionary partner, or even with my sister, unless I realize that I'm part of the larger Field of Intimacy and Desire.

There's no local intimacy that's local by itself. There's no local desire, which means that all of our intimacies have to contribute to the larger Field of Intimacy, and all of our desires have to contribute to the larger Field of Desire.

Therefore, what propels the Wheel of Co-Creation 2.0, is intimacy and desire. Wow! I am a unique configuration of desire and intimacy.

---

*I am a unique configuration of desire
and intimacy that is desired and loved
and needed by all of Reality.*

I want to add one piece here, which changes everything.

We're now going to go the next step, beyond Maslow. Maslow talked about a hierarchy of needs. His hierarchy of needs was pretty good. He did a great job. We're going to take the next step. I want to create a new vision of human needs. We can call this *Marc and Barbara's Hierarchy of Needs.* Abraham Maslow, wherever you are in the continuity of consciousness, you're going to love this.

There are six core human needs. **The first need is to be *intended*.** We have a need to be intended, which is why, if someone wakes up on your birthday and says, *Oh man, I just remembered it was your birthday. Happy Birthday*—that's okay. It's not too bad.

On the other hand, if they spent three weeks intending your birthday, or your anniversary, or whatever it is, or intending something, and you realize they did all this planning and intending, you are much more honored. You are much more moved. We need to be intended. That's the first core human need: I need to be intended.

Two, I need to be *recognized*. I need to be seen. We're all systematically misrecognized. We need to feel like we're recognized, we're seen for who we are, so we can liberate ourselves from the devastating sense of being invisible.

The need to be seen is not a need of the ego. It's not a narcissistic need.

- It's a fundamental need of a human being.
- It's a fundamental right of a human being.
- It's rooted in Divinity Herself. Divinity wants to be seen.

That's part of why Reality exists.

We want, desperately, to be seen and to be understood. That's how we are liberated from our loneliness.

So we have a second need, to be recognized.

We have a third need. **Our third need is to be *desired*, to be wanted.** That need to be desired is fundamental. It's so powerful that if we feel like we are not desired, or our partner or a friend moves their desire to someone else, we move into a murderous rage. We call it a crime of passion when someone kills someone because their partner desired someone else. It's not a crime of passion. It's a crime of the failure of passion. It's the failure of recognizing that I'm desired in a deeper way than just by my partner. But at least what we see from the story is a fundamental need to be desired. When we're not desired, we're crazed. We have a fundamental need to be desired—that's three.

The fourth need is to be *chosen*. We have a need to be *the one*. How we are chosen is a big question. One of the reasons that we're so committed to a particular context of relationship is it gives us the illusion of being chosen. If you're married to me, and we live in the same house, and you do sexuality only with me, then I'm chosen. But of course, it could mean many other things. It could mean that we have economic necessity. It could mean that I can't get out of it. It could mean that this is the cultural requirement. I can live with someone my whole life, have six kids, and never be chosen. We create those cultural constructs to be able to address that need to be chosen. We have a need to be chosen.

The fifth need is to be *adored*. Not just loved. Love is a word that has been overused. Adored means I am doting on you. I'm thinking about you all the time. We have a fundamental need to be adored.

The sixth need is to be *needed*. We need to be needed. We have now, according to the new field of psycho-neuro-immunology (that started thirty years ago), a situation where in a couple, when one passes, and the other doesn't have a larger sense of being needed, then the remaining spouse passes away soon after. We have a fundamental need to be needed.

Now, here is the gorgeousness of it. This is the core of the *dharma*. It's the core of the new humanity and the new human, the emergence of *Homo amor universalis*. **This is the core realization of *Homo amor universalis*:**

I do not exile those six core human needs to any one person.

Or to any two people, or any three people. That's not how it works.

Rather, in my very identity as *Homo amor universalis*, as Evolutionary Unique Self, I actually realize that I am intended. Reality intended me. When I can feel that, I get under my personality, and I have this experience of Reality intending your *you-ness*, before there was you—before you self-created—Reality is intending your *you-ness*.

When I feel that, I can rest for the first time. Reality recognizes. Reality sees. You are liberated into the recognition of Reality itself.

The meeting of these core human needs is implicit in the very definition of being a Unique Self. To be unique means that I was intended:

- Reality intended me.
- I am not a repetition. I am not a replication.
- I am a unique configuration of intimacy, intended by all of Reality.
- I'm a painting, with such dazzling precision, such beautiful colors woven together with such a specific, gorgeous background, with 50 trillion cells in utter, unique

complementarity that never were, are, or will be, present in this particular way ever again in all of eternity.

♦ I am intended. I experience myself as being intended.

I experience myself as being recognized. Just as a friend hears me talking, Reality hears me talking. I am heard; I'm recognized by Reality. When someone else recognizes me, they're participating in the larger Field of Reality's Recognition.

Not only that; let's go deeper. I am chosen. That's what uniqueness means. To be a *Homo amor universalis* means that I'm completely chosen by Reality itself. Reality has chosen me in this unique expression.

I'm adored. Reality is investing enormous energy and effort to sustain me at every moment. If I knew, if I would just wake up to the biological reality of the amount of energy that's going through my body—the amount of complex, infinite, dazzling attention going into sustaining me in every moment—I would be blown away. Oh my God, I am adored! Reality is pouring *unique presence* into me at every moment.

I am desired! How do I know I'm desired? Because the very Field of Reality is allurement. The very field, the cellular structure, the atomic structure that holds me together in every second is the desire of Reality. Every cell is allured. Every molecular particle is allured to another one. I'm literally a Field of Desire and allurement breathed by Reality in every second.

Finally, I'm needed. I'm needed by all of Reality. I have a unique gift to give. It can be given by no one who ever was, is, or will be other than me. That unique gift makes me participate and allows me to participate in the Unique Self Symphony. Which is the very mechanism for what we call the Planetary Awakening in Love through Unique Self Symphonies.

I am ultimately needed.

That's *Homo amor universalis*. That's the experience.

CHAPTER THREE

MY UNIQUE DESIRE IS GOD'S DESIRE: HEALING THE CRISIS OF DESIRE

Episode 103 — October 6, 2018

EVOLUTIONARY LOVE CODE: THE FIELD OF DESIRE

The Field of Intimacy is seamless but not featureless.

I am a unique expression of the larger Field of Intimacy and Desire.

I am a unique configuration of intimacy and desire.

Let's now place our attention on our own unique configuration of desire. See if you can get in touch with that configuration of desire that is uniquely yours. Feel that intimate desire within you to be an expression of the self-organizing Universe desiring through you. Where does the desire in you come from, except from the desire of universal evolution itself? The Universe is desiring through you and me; its desire can only be fulfilled through you and me. This is an awesome responsibility that everyone has: to fulfill their deepest heart's desire as an expression of the Universe itself.

PRAYER MEANS THAT THE PROCESS IS PERSONAL

What do we mean by prayer? My friend sometimes says to me, *I don't believe in God, but I believe in prayer*. What he means is **the god you don't believe in doesn't exist**, which is one of our sayings in Evolutionary Church.

Not the small god, the ethnocentric god, the god who is the *cosmic vending-machine god*, owned by only one religion, where you put in a quarter and you get out a shiny red something.

Not that god that says, *you are out and I am in.*

Not the god who is homophobic and really obsessed to make sure that you don't self-pleasure at night. Not that god.

I believe in prayer means to pray to the God who is the desire that animates all of Cosmos.

This is the very core idea that we are pointing to at the core of our memes:

Reality is desire.

When we say God, God equals Reality, but *not impersonal* Reality. Reality is not just impersonal, although one of its faces is impersonal; **Reality is personal**.

Here is a big sentence: **the process is personal**. It's not that there's the personal human thing and then there's the process which is impersonal beyond it. No, no, no, there's a personal human thing and an impersonal process that seems impersonal. But, when you get to the depth of that impersonal process, you realize it's all personal. The process itself is personal. The process itself is alive, living, conscious, intelligent. That process is not just a personal, Santa Claus god out there; it's actually the inherent intelligence of Cosmos which is *more* personal than we can imagine, not less personal.

The process knows our name. The process is not neutral. It's not a neutral process which is a bunch of mathematical formulas coming together in particular ways and *let's see what happens. There was a Holocaust, I guess that didn't work. That little Kosovo, that was a mess. Rwanda, uh!*

No, the process is inherently intelligent, and the process itself cries at the Holocaust. The process itself is devastated by the tragedy of Rwanda. The process knows our name. The process has desire. This is such a big idea. The way we say it in the original lineage mysticism is: Divinity desires.

What does Divinity desire? Divinity desires ever higher expressions of its own incarnation, the Good, the True and the Beautiful. Divinity desires ever higher manifestations of freedom, elegant order, and living consciousness of goodness, truth, and beauty. Because this intelligent process is so madly in love with Reality, She/He/It wants us to participate, to be It, to be divine miniatures. She manifests Herself, She contracts Herself into a point—*involution.* Then at the moment of Big Bang, she flares forth and begins to let her desire pour into Cosmos. **It's the desire for more depth, for more beauty, for more creativity, for more love.**

Whenever there's evil:

- It's a failure of love.
- It's a failure of intimacy.
- It's a failure of the basic desire of Cosmos which is for higher and deeper configurations of intimacy and love.

That desire lives in you. That's the turning point of today's church. That desire is alive in you.

When you find your own deepest heart's desire, which is at the core of the hub of the Wheel of Co-Creation 2.0, then you are actually locating divinity in yourself. That's what we do when we pray. When we pray, what are we doing? We're bringing our desires before God—that is what prayer is. We are saying, *God, this is my desire.* And God says, *Oh my God!* That's what God says.

What God says is, *Are you sure that is your deepest desire?*

We say, *Yeah, for sure man. That big red car, that's a "for sure"!*

But is there anything deeper?

Well, no, maybe a different model of car, okay?

A different model of car. I have that covered. Anything else?

God basically interrogates, tenderly, our desire and says, *give me your best shot. Give me your deepest desire—deeper. Is that all?*

We give God our deepest desire and God says, *give me deeper*, until we bring before the Divine our holy and our broken *Hallelujah*. Our deepest desire is not just universal peace, although that is there, but it's also my deepest desire that my daughter find her partner.

My deepest desire is that I can give my gift to the world.

My deepest desire is that I can have the stability of financial integrity so I can be free and spacious to give love to the world.

My deepest desires are intimate, personal, and specific.

The desire for my personal need is affirmed by the dignity of the infinite, conscious, intelligent Godhead who is evolution, who knows my name. That's what we're doing in prayer. We're finding our deepest desire.

When I find my deepest desire and I offer it before the Divine, the Divine becomes ecstatic, a paroxysm of delight and self-recognition. *Ahhhh! There I am! Yes! As you!* Reality is having a *you* experience. The Divine is just completely lit up with divine ecstasy that can only be offered through you, through me, speaking our deepest desire.

OUR COLLECTIVE DESIRE IS FOR EVOLUTIONARY LOVE

It's an awesome thought that my deepest heart's desire is the Universe's deepest heart's desire through me, as me, and *uniquely* as me. It was always

God is here desiring something and I have my own personal desire. If we understand that our heart's desire is coming straight from the nature of God itself through us, there's an enormous empowerment to desire that comes in.

I always say, of my own heart's desire, *what is it that I am really desiring?* In the broadest sense I find I'm desiring exactly what the 13.7 billion years of evolution desires: it desires greater consciousness.

Whatever our unique desire is, we all desire that inner impulse of consciousness itself.

The second great desire of universal creativity is *freedom*: freedom for everyone to be more fully and uniquely who we are. Here we're taking God's desire for freedom for the individual into our own ability to be free, through the consciousness of the impulse of creation. This is an enormous understanding of freedom.

Then the third part of God's desires through us is for *greater complexity or connectivity or love.* An ever more complex system, with ever greater connectivity of separate particles, making a new whole far greater than the sum of our parts. Let's put all of that in there.

What do we mean by Evolutionary Love? We've also called it Outrageous Love. **A synonym for Outrageous Love is Evolutionary Love. The only response to outrageous pain is Evolutionary Love in every one of us, which is Outrageous Love.**

The church of Evolutionary Love, perhaps for the first time ever, is for the fulfillment of the unique configuration of intimacy and desire, within its mission and within its members. So we enter the Evolutionary Church with our unique intimacy of desire, seeing it as Evolutionary Love along the pathway of the core of the spiral itself, at the very hub of the Wheel of Co-Creation desiring through us.

When Evolutionary Love is shared within a collective configuration, everyone's unique love goes through and beyond the True Self, through the

Unique Self into the Evolutionary Unique Self empowered by the intimacy of God desiring through you and through me. **When I connect my unique desire to God's desire, then I have to ask myself what is *truly* my heart's desire if I go the whole way with it in this lifetime.**

Let's each of us ask, right now within ourselves, *What is my deepest heart's desire?* This is in fact God desiring through me, going the whole way in this lifetime, joining with all others doing the same in a Unique Self Symphony of the birth of the new humanity in the new world. That's my deepest heart's desire: to go the whole way in this lifetime.

Why should we be going the whole way in this lifetime? Because this is the lifetime when God *has* to go through the whole way to create the next stage of life on Earth. If we don't go the whole way collectively in this lifetime, in this next twenty, fifty years, whatever it may be, the world *itself* cannot go the whole way.

We are the Evolutionary Church of going the whole way in this lifetime, being a beacon of light for people everywhere on Earth who are yearning to go the whole way. We're inviting them to be participants in the Evolutionary Church of love to fulfill the highest destiny of each of us, collectively and individually, for an awakening of a planet where all of our great new capacities are connected through us in a glorious celebration of the uniqueness of human creativity through God.

I HEAL GOD'S BROKEN HEART BY ACCESSING MY DEEPEST HEART'S DESIRE

I am just delighted! Let me speak from that delight because that delight is going to take us forward. Let's be in desire.

Where are we today in the world? What is the core crisis that underlies the ennui. Remember George Steiner? He was a great thinker and he talks about this ennui, this low-level sense of depression, this low-level deadness that we feel, this loneliness that is there, always, at the edges. It's the sense of, *is this the whole thing?* That feeling of dis-ease—what is the core? Where does it come from?

What we are saying, in these Evolutionary Love Codes, in the *dharma*, in this new evolution of the source code, in the post-postmodern, in the reconstructive project and the new story, what we are saying is that the core of the whole thing is a crisis of desire. **There is a crisis of desire.** The crisis of desire is that we can't feel our desire. We can't feel it!

When I can't feel my desire, I'm dead.

When I feel my desire, when I'm the full aliveness of my desire, do I ask myself what the meaning of life is? I don't think so. I am fully focused on my desire. Now, that of course has shadow and it has light.

I will just give you a simple example. I (Marc) remember when I was young, at the end of the *Yom Kippur* holiday, which is the Day of Atonement, the Day of At-onement, which is a 24-hour fast day. You come to synagogue on Friday night and you are into it. You are passionately praying. You're praying, but by the time it gets to about 4 o'clock in the afternoon, you're about 20 hours into the fast, and you're thinking about one thing: you are hungry. You would like to eat.

The last hour of the fast is ecstatic because you know you're about to eat. But there's this moment, from like 4:00 in the afternoon to about 7:00 in the evening where, whatever you are doing and praying, you're really just thinking about one thing: *I am really hungry.* The desire for food is at the center.

I remember being ten years old, and I remember noticing something important. I noticed, *Wow, I'm not sad about anything!* I was sad about a lot of things when I was a kid. I'm not sad about anything—about Mom or Dad, or all the stuff going on—when I have to eat. I was noticing that my desire for food, and all my thoughts about life and the meaning of life went into the background.

I remember being in fourth grade and making an oath to myself, in the middle of school, when I was being treated cruelly by other children. I didn't have the right glasses and I had patches in my pants. We brought down the average income in the school dramatically, and so on. This poor kid. I don't quite fit in. I'm the kind of butt of cruel jokes. I remember swearing, *I'm gonna remember and fight against cruelty when I get older. I swear I won't forget it.*

But then, all of a sudden, all that would disappear when I had this desire for food. All I wanted was to eat. That's a very deep thing. Meaning, when I have a clear desire, and that desire is a legitimate desire—it's about the very *being* of my lifeforce—then all the questions about the meaning of life fall away. All I want to do is fulfill my desire. It is ecstatic!

I remember being, again, nine, ten, eleven, twelve, thirteen when I started fasting. You always tried to do it, when you were a kid in Jewish Orthodoxy. You tried to start fasting at the age of ten to show that you were really in: *I can fast the whole day.*

I remember being disappointed when we finally ate, beloved Barbara, because then I didn't have the desire anymore. Then it was, *oh, now life is back to all of its usual pains. Really? This kind of sucks!* This is very deep. This is how we get that:

All of the dharma is written in our life experience.

Imagine that now my desire is not just for food but, as the prophet says, *not a hunger for food but a hunger for the word of God.*

Imagine that my desire is:

- For every child on the planet to be raised knowing that he or she is a unique configuration of intimacy and desire;
- That every child on the planet knows, *I am a Unique Self.*

- That every child on the planet knows there's a song only they can sing, there is a poem only they can write, there is a way of being, loving and living in the world that is theirs alone.
- That every child on the planet knows, *All of Reality desires me and yearns for my poem*, yearns for their contribution, yearns for their song, yearns for their heart's desire.

Reality's heart, the One Heart, yearns for my heart's desire because my heart is part of the One Heart. The shaman often says, before one begins a journey, *know that your heart is part of the One Heart*. My heart's desire is part of the One Heart.

Here is the deepest realization. That One Heart is broken. It's the broken heart of the Divine until I heal God's broken heart by accessing my heart's desire.

We're not just the church of Evolutionary Love; we're the church of evolutionary desire! Desire is sacred. What has happened is we've exiled desire. That's that statement of Buddha in the original Pali Canon, which I heard originally from a close friend of mine who was a Buddhist teacher: *Have few desires, but have great ones!*

MY UNIQUE DESIRE IS GOD'S DESIRE

When we don't do that, we get a pornographic internet, which is the nervous system of the planet, and, as the Broadway musical *Avenue Q* says, *the internet is for porn*, meaning *degraded desire*.

This is not beautiful erotica. Beautiful erotica has a place. The sexually intertwisted cherubs above the ark in the Holy of Holies. Beautiful erotica has a place.

Porn is not gorgeous Eros; it's a quick hit of degraded desire. It's not just degrading for women. It's degrading for men, women, and all consumers. No one signs their name triumphantly on their pornography.

Why am I talking about pornography? Oh my God! Because that's what happens:

When we can't access our great desires, we get an internet wired for degraded desire.

Our great desires should include everything. But if we're going to do physical desire, then do gorgeous Eros. Physical desire is just one expression. It's just the beginning. Our desires for food and for touch are the original desires that we live in.

But then we want to go deeper:

> We want not just food, but nourishment.
> We want not just touch, but to touch deeply into an idea.
> We want to touch deeply into our essence.

We want evolutionary desire, which is the evolution of our desire.

Where does our desire evolve to? Our desire evolves into God. We call it *apotheosis*. It is a fancy word. Apotheosis means *the great realization* that I participate in God. **God holds me: every place I fall, I fall into Her hands, and Her greatest desire is to hold me.** I am Her, at the same time.

What we do is, we shut down our desire, because we feel like, oh my God, I had my arms around the Universe and then my arms were ripped apart; my desires were left bloodied and rejected.

- We're afraid to speak our full desire.
- We're afraid to go the whole way in this lifetime.

We have to access the dignity of our desire. At the core of the ennui that laces our planet, that drenches our planet in shame, that drenches our planet in depression and degradation, that fails to allow us to envision the new evolution of the source code… is a crisis of desire.

Here in Evolutionary Church, we're owning the dignity of desire. *I am desire*. Let it rip. Let it light up the heavens since, together, we *are* desire. We are evolving the source code. I am not *just* desire—can we take this one step further? I am *unique* desire! That's the source of my dignity. **My unique desire is God's desire. When I get that, the crisis of desire is healed.**

My friends, dear, holy, gorgeous friends, what is the *MeToo* crisis if not a crisis of desire? It's the demonization of male desire. It's male desire acted out in ways that are inappropriate and boundary crossing.

But why are men acting out? Men are acting out because they can't find their deepest desire, and women are split off. Women are acting out, and women are split off from their own deepest desire. They don't know how to access the dignity of desire at all levels and in all forms. They don't know how to take agency and power over their desire.

The truth is that we all desire.

Our deepest desire, our deepest heart's desire, is God's desire, and we are all desired.

That's the core. Just feel this. Our core *dharma*. What does it mean to be a Unique Self, an Evolutionary Unique Self, a *Homo amor universalis*?

What it means is knowing that:

- I am intended. Reality intends me.
- I am chosen. Reality chooses me.
- Reality recognizes me.
- Reality adores me.
- Reality needs me.

Drumroll in the heavens! Reality desires me! The dignity of desiring and the dignity of being desired.

That is what we want.

What do we desire? We desire to know what love is. I want to know what love is. We all have felt heartache and pain. But, oh my God, we've traveled so far—we can't stop now. We're going to know what love is together. Love is Evolutionary Love.

Love is to love it open all the way.

That's what we're committed to do here, a band of Outrageous Evolutionary Lovers in Evolutionary Church.

CHAPTER FOUR

HEALING THE CRISIS OF INTIMACY: FALLING MADLY IN LOVE WITH OURSELVES AS UNIQUE CONFIGURATIONS OF DESIRE AND INTIMACY

Episode 104 — October 13, 2018

EVOLUTIONARY LOVE CODE: EVERY CRISIS IS A CRISIS OF INTIMACY

Our crisis is a birth, personally and collectively, because crisis is an evolutionary driver.

Every great crisis, at its root, is a crisis of intimacy.

Crisis means that someone or something is being left out of our circle.

INCREASING INTIMACY MEANS BRINGING IN WHAT IS LEFT OUT OF THE CIRCLE

In every crisis, ask yourself the question: *what is being left out of the circle?* The solution to the crisis is a new configuration of intimacy.

43

Let's place our attention on someone or something we are leaving out of our circle of intimacy, creating some crisis in our lives. Just imagine that. Can you think of someone you're leaving out of your circle? Feel the crisis and pain that's resulting from that. Now invite into the circle whoever has been excluded from your circle of intimacy, and feel the pain dissolve as they experience this intimacy increasing.

It's so easy to take for granted but, the fact is:

- We're here.
- We're able to serve.
- We're able to love.
- We're able to participate in evolving the source code.

This is true even before any word comes out of our mouths, just by opening our hearts all the way.

Let's look at this wonderful code:

Our crisis is a birth, personally and collectively, because crisis is an evolutionary driver.

Every great crisis, at its root, is a crisis of intimacy.

A crisis means that something is being left out of the circle.

The solution, the way you heal the crisis, is you figure out what has been left out, and you bring it back in.

Earlier we pointed to an example: *is there someone left out of my circle or is there something left out of me?* In other words, *what am I not bringing to the table?* There's always a part of me that I'm not bringing to the table because of a failure of self-love. There's a part of me that thinks that I'm a deplorable. *I'm a deplorable!* Somehow, there's a part of me that's not really loving myself: *If people only knew that dark thought.*

We're always leaving *the deplorables* out. When we leave the deplorables out, whether that's politically, or personally, then what the deplorables do is, they take the wheel. They take the steering wheel because they're so furious.

When we pray, we invite the holy and broken *Hallelujah*.

What is our holy and our broken *Hallelujah*?

- It's our gorgeousness and our *deplorable*.
- It's our hurt and our halo.
- It"s our wonder and our lack of wonder.

Just feel in the moment. I'm all about transformation. **I'm all about standing in integrity and being the utter best I can be, but I have to start from a place of compassion.** Life is hard. The world loves, and the world hurts. We're gorgeous, and we get hurt. We get hurt a lot.

---

*Life is about transmuting that hurt,
transmuting the broken Hallelujah
into the holy Hallelujah.*

Life is about taking the outrageous pain and turning it into Outrageous Love.

Life is about taking the descent and turning it into the ascent.

It's about taking loneliness and turning it into love.

I want to just really hold the deplorable, the place where we weren't the best that we could be. The place that we didn't show up. The place where we said something that slid out of our mouth, that was not our highest self. We responded to something that someone else said with a sense of contraction, or clench. We all clench.

You know the place of the clench? We have all felt the clench. The clench is when your heart closes.

I (Marc) had, this morning before I came to church, I had a difficult exchange with someone who has been a deep, creative partner for many years. The exchange worked fine in the end. They broke through my Sabbath barrier with some set of urgencies. The exchange was fine, but I was left with this sense of clench. I was angry. I knew I was angry, not just about that exchange, I was angry about this broader sense of injustice I had. Then I felt, *Wow, I am taking that person out of my heart. I can't take that person out of my heart. In my mind, even though I'm being loving and saying all the right things, I'm making them into a deplorable; I'm angry at them.*

I had to step out of that, take their perspective, hold on to mine, and feel what they felt—I still think they're wrong. I think that their position is incorrect, but I could feel them. I could also feel the hurt and the trauma in their own life that led them to make a series of decisions that I think were wrong.

I'm going to hold the integrity of my position. I'm not going to say *multiple perspectives*. I think I'm right, and they're wrong, but I stopped making them *deplorable*. I *get* their pain. I can hold that. I can hold the tension in it without needing to make someone a deplorable. The same thing about ourselves: there's a little part of ourselves that we've split off and made deplorable.

A SIMPLE PRACTICE OF UNCLENCHING AND OPENING THE HEART

I just want to invite everyone to unclench. It's a simple thing. I do this all day. If you had a little secret mirror or camera in my office, you would see me doing this all day. I go like this: **I take my hand, I put it on my heart, like it was a door, and I open it.** I walk around doing that all day. It's true.

What I'm doing is a little action, a simple ritual, to open my heart. It's so easy to close our hearts. We can be really effective and say meaningful things all day to people, but our heart is closed. We are on automatic pilot. We're just doing what we do.

- To live with an open heart doesn't mean not to be fierce.
- It doesn't mean not to take positions.
- It doesn't mean not to act, sometimes with audacity, sometimes in ways, that are hard.

It means I'm always doing it with an open heart.

There are no deplorables on the other side. **When you make someone into a deplorable, they** *become* **a deplorable.** When you make yourself into a deplorable, then you stop loving yourself; and the deplorable—without you even realizing it is happening—takes the steering wheel of your life.

This is a moment for radical self-love, knowing that, wow, it hurts. There are holy and broken *Hallelujahs*. We can all feel the tears welling up. We have all been able to show up in a thousand ways, and there are ways in which we haven't shown up in the deepest way we wanted to. That's okay. We are going to do better, starting today.

When we come before God in prayer, we embrace the deplorable, bring the holy and the broken *Hallelujah*, and say:

> *God, wow! What a world you have created! It's so gorgeous. It's so stunning. It's so outrageously beautiful!*
>
> *And what were you thinking? It's so painful, also! But I trust you, and as I'm committed to the evolution of love, to unclenching, to opening my heart, I bring before you, in this moment, my holy and my broken Hallelujah.*

THE SELF-ORGANIZING UNIVERSE DESIRES MORE INTIMACY

How do you think this Universe was formed? This is the most amazing story. It is true that evolution *desires* intimacy, but evolution also *creates* intimacy. Just think, for a moment, of the origin of creation. Cast your mind back to the explosion of this evolutionary spiral.

Out of that come quarks, electrons, protons, neutrons, cells, multi-cells, animals, and humans. What happens at every turn of the spiral? Separate parts are brought together to create a greater whole, far greater than the sum of their parts.

In other words, the self-organizing universe, the invisible process of creation, has the tendency, the capacity, the genius to connect particles together, by what?

By attraction, by desire.

The Universe is a love story. **Our crisis is the birth of a greater and more complex species.**

Let's just imagine this attraction. Now, if the Universe is self-organizing for 13.7 billion years, let's take it into the heart of our life, right this second. The genius of the entire self-organizing Universe has entered your heart.

What is it doing there? It's connecting separate particles together: All the parts of your desire, all the parts we might feel are deplorable, all the people you love that might be left out of your life, or that might be hurt by you, or those you are hurt by. Call upon the genius of the self-organizing Universe, right now, to bring coherence into your heart. It may be hard to imagine that the self-organizing Universe, which created ever more complex systems, is now entering your life.

First of all, imagine your life as the self-organizing genius of the Divine connecting all your separate parts, so you're becoming whole. **That wholeness of your being is your genius, brought together by the genius of the self-organizing Universe.**

Now, imagine the Evolutionary Church being filled with the movement of the self-organizing universe, connecting every one of us with one another in an intimate union of love, creativity, and desire for the church itself to fulfill its members. Our very participation in this community is evoking the self-organizing Universe. We put our hands on our hearts and open the door. We're connecting the hundreds and thousands of people who are part of our collective.

Imagine us calling on the self-organizing Universe to evolve and connect this church into the radiant presence of love that it is already, and that Universe within us is self-organizing.

Let's take another step, beyond our church. Let's imagine the leaders of this world who are struggling with the nation-states, who are struggling in the United Nations, who are struggling with these tremendously difficult climate change problems, all trying to remain in power while separated by competition and despair.

Imagine, for a moment, the self-organizing Universe that brought together the quarks, electrons, protons, cells, and all of us for 13.7 billion years. It's surely not stopping now! If you can imagine the spiral of the Wheel of Co-Creation 2.0. You see every sector of that wheel there—health, education, economics, science and technology, and all the rest.

Imagine now that we're gathering together as an expression of the self-organizing Universe, of our culture, as depicted in the Wheel of Co-Creation 2.0. It would be an enormous explosion of energy.

Now, since we're one with the self-organizing Universe, and knowing that its truly greatest desire is a planetary awakening in love through a Unique Self Symphony—through a unique jazz symphony with everyone who is attracted to do this—we can imagine the same self-organizing Universe holding the power to attract everyone into our collective vision for humanity. From that depth of perspective, we can imagine a planetary awakening in love.

Because we live at the crisis of the sixth mass extinction, because nature has brought us to this very point of devolution or conscious evolution, this is the moment when it's possible for the yearning of greater intimacy to jump into a higher order.

As we stated in our code, *our crisis is a birth*. Our intimacy is the desire of the Universe to connect. God desires intimacy for billions of years and God is in us, desiring it now. The self-organizing Universe is working through each of our deepest heart's desires to heal the pain, to overcome the separation and to say, *we have the purpose*, perhaps never brought together quite like this before on Earth, *for a planetary awakening in love through our Unique Self Symphony.*

SELF-LOVE IS THE KEY TO HEALING THE GLOBAL INTIMACY DISORDER

Let the fire of the evolutionary impulse come down and open our hearts. Let's weave this together. I want to go so deeply into this with you.

This code says that *every crisis is a crisis of intimacy,* and we're living today in a global intimacy disorder. **We have to heal the global intimacy disorder through an evolution of intimacy.** Evolution desires intimacy and evolution manifests intimacy. That's the nature of evolution. That which creates intimacy, creates new intimacy, meaning it creates new emergence.

What does new intimacy mean? New intimacy means something that was left out of the circle is now brought into the circle.

Really feel this! **When I don't have real intimacy and I want to be in the circle, what do I do? I create pseudo-intimacy. So, what do I do? I leave something outside of the circle, or someone outside of the circle. That's who I referred to as** *the deplorables.*

We leave those people out of the circle. They're out of the circle, and that gives me an illusion that I'm in the circle—that's pseudo-eros.

Eros, or intimacy, means *I'm in the circle.*

But when I'm not in the circle, I have to make somebody else outside the circle to give me the illusion that I am in the circle. But once I'm actually inside the circle, I'm filled with Eros.

Here is the deepest truth: there is truly room for everyone inside.

If you're actually inside, yourself, there's room for everybody inside. That's the deepest truth. The deepest truth of Reality is that when you're on the inside, there's room for everyone. The question is, *can I actually step inside?*

The way I step inside is not through a superficial self-acceptance.

It's not through failing to challenge myself.

It's not that I'm not inviting myself to transform. I continue to invite myself to transform.

It's not that I'm not moving from my victim story to my hero story—I *do* continue to move to my hero story.

That's all happening, but, what it means is that the core experience of self-love, of intimacy with myself, is the realization that *all of Reality was worth manifesting for my sake*. This is a very deep truth. It's important that we get this.

If we get it on the surface, it's narcissism, or it's an ego run amok.

But, if I get it in the deepest place, then *the whole world changes*. When I'm on the inside, when I'm in that state of being on the inside,

- ◆ I realize that I'm so valuable, I'm so gorgeous, I'm so stunningly beautiful, that every flutter of my heart matters in the calculus of eternity.
- ◆ I feel eternity breathing and loving me open in every second.
- ◆ I feel and know that the cascading movements inside of me.

and the fluctuations inside of me, are happening inside the mind of God and the mind of eternity itself.

- ◆ I know that I matter beyond imagination,
- ◆ I know, as the Hebrew mystics said, *bishvili nivra ha-olam*— the world was created for me, and the way that Hebrew translates, it also means: for the sake of my path, it was worth creating the world.

That, my friends, is the enlightenment experience.

In every great enlightenment tradition, the world over, **there are two demarcating characteristics to the *experience* of enlightenment.**

One is that I'm not separate from everything. I'm part of the All. I am part of the seamless coat of the Universe. The illusion of what Gregory Bateson called *a skin-encapsulated ego* is exploded. The optical delusion of consciousness is overcome.

That's the first part of the enlightenment experience, and it is huge. To have that experience, that I'm not just a separate self, that I'm with All, and I am part of the All. I can feel it at this moment, right now. When I'm not speaking from my personal *I-ness*, I'm speaking from the center itself. That's the first dimension of enlightenment.

But there's a second dimension of enlightenment. This is so deep. It's the deepest of the deep, the Inside of the Inside, the Holy of Holies: **When I'm in enlightenment, I also feel that it's all inside of me.**

That is not narcissism. Narcissism is when I feel that I'm deplorable, and so I cover up my hidden self-hatred—perhaps this is the love I didn't get from my father. I'm covering up something very deep and hidden with this sense of privilege and impulsiveness and primadonna-ness and overbearingness. *I'm entitled*, that's narcissism.

Narcissism comes from a failure of self-love.

But when you can feel that failure of self-love, and then you fall madly in love with yourself, something else happens.

I talk about falling madly in love with everyone; this week is about falling madly in love with yourself. You have to be madly in love with yourself. To be madly in love with yourself is not narcissism. Narcissism is when you hate yourself, but you have covered it up with ego. To be madly in love with yourself and know that you're worthy of self-love is intimacy.

In the code, we said that *every crisis is a birth, personally and collectively*. If every country were truly, madly in love with itself, they would have room for every other country. If Democrats were madly in love with Democrats they would see all the beauty and good intention of the Republicans. Yes, I did just say that! We would not make Judge Kavanaugh[1] a deplorable villain. If Republicans were really in love with themselves and their vision, then they would not have to make the Democrats the deplorables. **Polarization means, *I don't even want you around!* That polarization lives in me, so I have to fall in love with myself.**

Today I want to invite something: let's fall madly in love with ourselves. *Madly* means, it's beyond reason. Madly doesn't mean angry. It means *I'm madly in love with you*. The word *fully* is too tepid for me.

When you read Hafiz, or you read Rumi, or you read the Kabbalists, they talk about being *madly in love*. Madly in love means: *I'm ecstatic, I'm excited, I'm elated, I'm delighted, and I'm going to push through every boundary of contraction and smallness to express that love, to be with that love.*

---

1 Brett Michael Kavanaugh is an American lawyer and jurist serving as an Associate Justice of the Supreme Court of the United States. He was nominated by President Donald Trump on July 9, 2018, and has served since October 6, 2018.

That's what we call Outrageous Love.

The word *rage* is negative, but we're referring rather to the linguistic root of rage, which is *wild, ecstatic delight and feeling*. When I'm not madly in love with myself, when I'm not outrageously in love with myself, then I'm raging at other people because I'm trying to find a way to be alive and to find myself.

I want to be really precise about this.

The crisis of intimacy means I have left too much of myself out. I have this hidden failure of self-love.

Our prayer is to be madly in love with ourselves. When I'm madly in love with myself, I'm madly in love with all the people around me. We can be madly in love with each other.

When you fall madly in love with yourself, then you fall madly in love with everyone. And again, when we say *madly in love* here, we don't mean romantically, that's one very narrow band of love. **We mean Evolutionary Love, Outrageous Love: the love that isn't mere human sentiment, but the heart of existence itself.** We're here together with this shared purpose.

Can we really say, *I'm madly in love with myself*? Can we do that? It's not so easy, is it?

Let's feel it: *I'm madly in love with myself.* Don't skip it. Remember, the crisis of intimacy means I've left myself outside of the circle: *I want to fall madly in love with someone else because I am not madly in love with myself.* So, I open my heart, and I realize, *oh my God, I'm madly in love with myself.*

Sometimes we have to put a cap on ourselves because sometimes people can't handle it, but when I'm madly in love with myself, I'm willing to go the whole way in this lifetime.

Sometimes we go too quickly to, *I love myself with abundance that overflows into the world.* We automatically make sure to include the world. Let's totally be dedicated to the world, but first be sure you can say, *I'm madly in love with myself.*

I want to give it to you in evolutionary terms. In evolutionary terms we talk about a *survival drive.* I have a drive to survive. You can read the literature of evolutionary psychology, and you will see it will talk about some beautiful human drive, let's say for music, and it will say, *but that is really not an expression of Spirit, but merely a survival drive,* as if the drive for survival explains Spirit away. They say, *oh, that's a drive for survival.*

Let's look into this more deeply. What is survival? Survival is a *telos,* a purpose.

The second you realize that evolution has a purpose, you're no longer in materialism—you're in the God realm, in the Divine realm.

To say *I'm madly in love with myself* is a huge deal. To say *I want to survive* is actually just the exterior of being madly in love with myself. Because why do I want to survive?

> Why do we have a drive to survive?
> Who put that drive to survive in me?
> Why are we wired for survival?
> Why is survival such a huge given?

Survival is a given because there's an interior *telos* which says we want more life, and I'm particularly responsible to have more of *my* life in the Universe. That's what the survival drive means.

The survival drive means, and here is the big sentence:

Survival drive is the exterior of self-love (which is the interior).

That changes all of evolutionary thought.

This drive for survival, which everyone acknowledges—what is that? That is the exterior form in which I say, **there has to be more of myself in the world.** There has to be more (*insert your name here*)—the world needs my uniqueness.

When you say, *the world needs my uniqueness, so I have to survive,* that's the drive to survive; that's actually self-love. That's being madly in love with myself.

- When you're actually in love with yourself—I'm gonna tell you a crazy secret—everyone wants to hang out with you.
- When you're a narcissist, no one wants to hang out with you.

Being madly in love with yourself means you're inviting everyone else to be madly in love with themselves as well. Wow!

This insight we just gave about survival critiques the entire literature of evolutionary psychology and shows its great weakness. That literature is not acknowledging there is a *telos,* meaning there's a purpose built into the story, and that is survival of *you.* You're the chairman of the board responsible for the survival of your unique quality of life force in Reality. You can do that for real only if you're madly in love with yourself. Isn't that unbelievable? Isn't that gorgeous?

The self-organizing Universe organizes through my *self.* My *self* that organizes the self-organizing Universe is the configuration of intimacy that is me. All of Reality is heading for self-termination now because we have exponentialized our growth. We're about to fall off the cliff, because complicated systems always break down. But what we know, and this is a distinction that complexity theorist Dave Snowden[2] makes:

Nature creates *complex systems* (cellular reproduction is a complex system), whereas human beings, at least until now, have

---

2 David John Snowden is a Welsh management consultant and researcher in the field of knowledge management and the application of complexity science.

created *complicated systems*. That's a very important distinction in evolutionary theory.

A complex system is a system in which the connection between the parts is not artificial; it is based on attraction, on allurement. That's a very important distinction. When we create artificial connection, it breaks down. Reality itself manifests incredible connectivity, based on this constant attraction. That's what *The Universe: A Love Story* means.

In order for us human beings to participate as divine partners and to create not complicated systems but complex systems, we have to access our self that is the configuration of the Infinity of Intimacy alive in me. Then we'll be able to manifest complex systems.

CHAPTER FIVE

CRISIS IS AN EVOLUTIONARY DRIVER: OUR COLLECTIVE AWAKENING TO REALITY MADLY IN LOVE WITH US

Episode 105 — October 20, 2018

EVOLUTIONARY LOVE CODE: NEW CONFIGURATIONS OF INTIMACY

Our crisis is a birth, personally and collectively, because our crisis is an evolutionary driver.

Every great crisis is, at its root, a crisis of intimacy. Crisis means that someone or something is being left out of the circle.

In every crisis, ask yourself the question, what's being left out of the circle?

The solution to the crisis is a new configuration of intimacy within the circle.

REALITY IS MADLY IN LOVE WITH ME

We are here at the threshold of the greatest crisis that the world has ever seen collectively, which is the planet crisis. And there's no way that the climate crisis can be solved without the intimacy of people on the planet

experiencing themselves as part of a whole living system. Let's place this crisis as the birth of a universal global humanity. That's the truth.

We're now experiencing, in this church, a microcosm of a planetary reality. Let's hold here that our intimacy and our experiencing ourselves is part of a whole living system in which every member of this church is connected to every other member, so we can be a microcosm of a planetary birth that will affect a planetary crisis larger than we have ever seen before.

I'm so excited to be alive, and I'm so delighted to be with you!

One of the things we leave outside the circle is our joy. We wait for our joy when something happens that makes us happy. You say to someone, *are you happy today?* And they say, *well, what happened today to make me happy?* Really? Oh my God. Here we are! We're awake! Alive!

We have fifty trillion irreducibly, gorgeous, unique cells dancing in complementarity and brilliance beyond imagination, beyond what any supercomputer could manifest. The infinite Source of Reality itself that powers all power in the world, beyond imagination, is powering us, uniquely, in a way that no one else is powered. *Reality*, to paraphrase Meister Eckhart, *is kissing us open, personally, every second.* Reality is madly in love with me, personally.

Last week we talked about being madly in love with ourselves—loving those parts of ourselves we leave outside of the circle. **The second thing that we leave out of the circle is the idea that Reality is madly in love with me.** That's actually true. It's just a fact that we leave out of the circle.

In order to get your place in the whole story, and in order to talk about how to solve a world crisis—which is by ensuring everybody is on the inside— you must first, be madly in love with yourself and second, get that Reality is madly in love with you.

First, I can't leave out the fact that I'm madly in love with myself, and second—and this is so deep—I have to know that Reality is madly in love with me.

I will tell you why. Imagine when you know that your partner, your friend, your community, your brother, your sister, your romantic partner, your Outrageous Love partner is madly in love with you. When you know that your partner is madly in love with you then you can live in that little apartment, with not quite enough room, and you're fine.

But if no one is madly in love with you, then you can be living somewhere beautiful, have the biggest house in the world, have a huge trust fund, the most ample resources in the world—and there's *no room for you in the world.*

When there's no room for you in the world, then you try to take up more room, room that actually belongs to other people. Do you get what I'm saying? **When I experience Reality as being madly in love with me then I can take up my exact space in the world. I can use the exact resources that I need.**

I don't need a carbon footprint because *I have a soul print.*

Do you get what I am saying? It's really deep.

We think we can solve the climate crisis, but we can't solve it unless we ourselves are so on the inside that we realize that we're all on the inside *together*, and that no one left out.

A PRACTICE FOR ENTERING ON THE INSIDE

We are weaving together. Our intention here is for the sake of the evolution of love. It's a phrase that we brought down, maybe fifteen years ago. We are for the sake of the evolution of love. Here is how we do it: I get so inside myself.

How do I get inside?

Not only am I in love with myself, I realize that Reality is personally in love with me. That's the truth, and it's important to know:

The truth of my atomic structure, and its utter uniqueness.

The truth of my biological structure, and its utter uniqueness.

The truth of the unique structure of my mind, and its utter uniqueness, all before culture even begins to play.

Reality intends that uniqueness.

When I get that Reality is madly in love with me, even though I'm having a bad hair day, and even if I didn't get a trust fund, and I might be living in a little place—my soul print, my Unique Self print, lives and breathes and is seen in the world.

When we're all inside like that, then we can engage and transform and bring heaven on Earth.

I invite you into a special prayer, and I like to invoke the holy and broken *Hallelujah* of Leonard Cohen. One of the things that Leonard Cohen knew—he knew this lineage well—is that Reality is madly in love with me. Therefore, you always feel that no matter what is going on with him, Leonard Cohen is beyond shame.

That's why I like Leonard Cohen: he's beyond shame. He still holds appropriate regret. He can feel guilty, and he takes full responsibility. **Leonard Cohen is always accountable, but he's never lost in shame because he always has this experience that *Reality is madly in love with me.***

With all the women that Leonard Cohen loved—and there were a lot of them, as he wasn't doing the classical monogamy path—he always felt Reality loving him through other people.

I want to invite you to access a little bit of Leonard here for a second. Let's realize Reality is madly in love with me. God is looking at me directly and personally knowing me. From that place, ask God, *would you please give me a sign that you're madly in love with me?* This is a very special mystical practice, an advanced practice. You can't do it at a low level. The sign is usually not a red car! That's not how it works. It's so much more interesting.

Our lives matter because God, Reality, the Infinity of Intimacy is madly in love with us. So nothing is left out. Then, turn to God in prayer and ask for everything. *God, can you please give me a personal, intimate sign that Reality, that You, God, that You are madly in love with me?*

Then, as you go through the week, observe the intimate sign that you might have received this week. We're setting the ground to heal climate change. This is directly related. You can't do one without the other.

THE CLIMATE CRISIS IS AN EVOLUTIONARY DRIVER

I know not only does God love me, but God asks everything of me. That's part of God loving me and me asking everything of God. **When you realize that God loves you, God asks everything of you.** What does it feel like when God asks everything of you? It feels like everything that you are, and will be, and can be, and yearn to be, is to be given to the highest possibility of your life for the sake of God's love for you.

When we know that God loves us, then we also must love God. There's a reciprocal quality of being loved this much by God. It's that you love God, totally.

I read the climate change article in *Rolling Stone* about the fact that we're at the threshold of the annihilation of human civilization, unless the entire world changes its behavior pattern, together. This is awesomely large. God is asking this of all of us.

We've heard about this a lot but, somehow, this *Rolling Stone* article did it for me:

> A new report from the United Nations intergovernmental panel on climate change, the gold standard of climate science, outlines in frightfully stark terms what it would take to keep Earth's temperature below (a rise of) 1.5 degrees Celsius. What would this take to avoid a collapse of the rainforest, the coral reefs, the

melting of the ice sheet that would swamp coastal cities around the world, in heat extreme?

It is not enough that Portland, Oregon or Berkley, California gets to zero emissions by 2050 or the entire state of California, for that matter, or even the entire United States.

The entire world must eliminate, or offset carbon pollution by 2050s. It is like a deafening, piercing smoke alarm going off in the kitchen. We have to put out the fire.[3]

As I was thinking about how much God loves me, and how much I love God, basically God said to me, *what will you be doing about this?* I can say this to everybody in church, *what will you be doing about this?*

What has happened is that the intimate has become global. I'm also thinking here of the purpose of our church, which we've called, ultimately, *a Planetary Awakening in Love through a Unique Self Symphony* of everybody's voice, heard; or a jazz symphony in which we can play together. The goal of our church, not only symbolically, is the only hope for humanity to continue in the development of a civilization. The message that apparently is given here is that nobody can be left out of this challenge. It's not enough for a few small groups of people or advanced states, or networks of a few people to do this. We've never had such a thing. We've never been given such a thing.

Crisis precedes transformation.

We not only have our personal crisis, but we have a planetary crisis that we all know about. It's very well documented. Problems are evolutionary drivers. We're going to ask ourselves, *what does this one drive us towards?*

3 Jeff Goodell, "Can Earth Survive Climate Change?" *Rolling Stone*, October 9, 2018, https://www.rollingstone.com/politics/politics-news/can-earth-survive-climate-change-735067.

Nature takes quantum jumps. This is really interesting, according to intimacy. Nature takes quantum jumps by connecting separate parts to make a new, more comprehensive whole, greater than the sum of the parts. In other words: *nature is calling us.*

The Universe is a love story. Allurement and attraction starts with quarks, and extends all the way up to us.

Now, apparently the Universe is saying to us, *folks, we're talking about the planet! We're not just talking about Portland, Oregon, or Berkley, California!*

Here is what I (Barbara) have learned from my study of doing all those Syncons in the early 1970s and 1980s. **How does nature take these jumps? It does this by connecting separate parts so that innovations and creativity of one part are needed by the other part.**

It jumps by everyone saying, *yes, I'm responding to this. I want to give my innovation, my own best creativity to anyone who most needs it. And I want to receive other people's innovations that I most need. In other words:*

Synergistic convergence leads to emergence of the radically new.

I think it would be so exciting for us to practice synergistic convergence as a microcosm of a planetary response to climate change. Now, that may be a big jump of thought here but, apparently, the response to climate change can be handled only if the world itself comes together and deals with the pollution crisis *as a planet.* **That's what we have been dreaming of in some very deep way, in our hearts: our crisis being the birth of a planetary society capable of connecting all its parts to make a whole.**

I believe that through evolutionary collectives we could do a practice in which everybody is in touch with the greatest gift that they're yearning to give to others, and what they feel they most need from each other, that would make a huge difference in our hearts.

So here is the question to ask yourself: What is the greatest gift you would like to give to others—one that, in giving it, would make the greatest difference to you? And, if you want, add what you most need for somebody to give to you.

This is the question to practice synergistic convergence, because here is the truth: nature takes jumps by doing that. Nature creates new entities altogether by doing that for billions and billions of years.

We all wake up when we hear God asking us, *well, what are you going to do about this?*

This is the first thing I'm doing about it. Say what it is that you're most desirous of giving as a microcosm of a planetary society awakening in love. The way that nature does it is that if it happens somewhere, it can happen anywhere!

We can each be a model, and by putting it in the context of climate change as a threat to planetary civilization, I'm suggesting that **without a crisis of this order, a planetary awakening in love would never happen.**

This crisis is actually the evolutionary driver for the awakening of a planetary humanity. Without it we're going down into devolution, destruction, and the misuse of power, the whole way.

THE SOLUTION TO EVERY GREAT CRISIS IS NEW AND DEEPER INTIMACY

Can we feel this together? Let's bring back the code:

> Our crisis is a birth, personally and collectively, because crisis is an evolutionary driver. Every great crisis, at its root, is a crisis in intimacy. Crisis means that something, or someone, is being left out of the circle. Enlightenment means intimacy with all things—intimacy with all persons and things; intimacy with all parts of ourselves. Enlightenment means that there are no externalities.

When someone is missing from the circle, then we can't do it.

The solution to every great crisis is a new and deeper configuration of intimacy.

What happens is that we have something called a blind spot. I want you to notice this because this is where the rubber hits the road. This is where the work is. The blind spot means there's something in the way of me giving my gift, something I can't see.

What we tell ourselves, when our blind spot blocks us, or creates havoc in the world, is, *oh, that wasn't me.* We figure out why everyone else is to blame. And often, we're right. Sometimes there are people who behave as bad actors in the world. That's true. In other words, a hundred million people were killed in the twentieth century, people who were non-combatants, because there were bad actors.

Bad actors emerge from ordinary people, beautiful babies, who grow up as bad actors because they feel like they have no Eros. They're not inside the circle. The only way they can be inside the circle is to place someone else outside the circle.

Now let's look at ourselves for a second. I want to go deep with you. What we do is, we tell ourselves that we're not responsible because we have a blind spot. We tell ourselves that we're innocent. We don't ask ourselves, *what, in myself, have I left outside the circle of myself?*

When we said last week, *I'm madly in love with myself,* I don't want to be madly in love with a distorted vision of myself. I need to ask myself, *what in me am I blind to?* That's really important. *I was blind, and now I can see,* says the great English songwriter. *I was blind but now I see.* It's only when I see my blind spot that I can see how:

- I push people away.
- I create lack of trust.
- I'm grasping.

- I'm being impulsive.
- I set people up against each other by not creating a coherent circle.
- I may be a major contribution to lack of intimacy.
- I might be a major contribution to failures of intimacy.

We have to see that, without getting angry at or judging ourselves. Instead, say, *I'm committed to facing everything and avoiding nothing.*

It's only when I'm face-to-face with myself that I madly love all of myself. I hold myself. I hold myself and I love myself. I say, *Wow! I get where I was hurt in my early years, and then I get why I developed this as a trauma response and have been acting out unconsciously, and I'm going to bring that unconscious part that was outside of the circle back into the circle.* That"s really deep.

You might be thinking, *what does that have to do with climate change?* The answer is *everything!*

I want to get that with you. *Everything!*

We will not solve climate change unless we can all work together.

What does it mean that we're all going to work together? It means that all the individual egos, skin-encapsulated egos, who are running NGOs, who are the leading politicians, who are thought leaders, will **give up whatever their particular egoic need for success is—success of their brand, or a particular dimension of their political career, or whatever it may be— and act for the good of the whole.**

You can do that only if you're madly in love with yourself and you know that Reality is madly in love with you. If you can see your foibles and your weaknesses, work with them, love them, fall, and then get up again, and you engage again—then you're madly in love with all of yourself. You get that Reality is madly in love with you, and because you have that security, you can rest in it. From there, you can act audaciously.

It's not going to work if we bypass. We're at the moment in history where the only thing that's going to change, that's going to cause the evolution of love, is if I'm madly in love with myself, meaning *all* of myself. The blind spot can now be seen.

I'm not unconscious. I'm not innocent. Stop being innocent. Instead, recognize when *I am guilty! Guilty as charged! I made a mistake! I'm sorry. I'm accountable.*

Then claim what I call your "second innocence." Then we re-virginate. Not first innocence, but what we call second innocence, meaning I see everything. I have full accountability, full power, madly loving myself and then I claim my second innocence.

That's wisdom. That's power. I can do that if I realize that Reality's madly loving me. This is not a metaphor, it's not a poetic phrase—it's the truth.

Reality directly sees me in this moment and knows me.

Reality has conspired, has breathed in and breathed out time and again, to manifest the unique intention of me.

Once that's true, then I can begin to be heroic. I can start with what Campbell is famously cited for. By the way, everyone cites him, but no one does it right. Usually it's, *I want to go on a hero's journey, but I don't want to go through the dark night of the soul. I don't want to go into the cave. I don't want to do the work. I just want to go on the hero's journey.*

Every one of us is a spokesperson for Reality. I can't be a world spokesperson unless I do the work to be madly in love with myself and know that Reality is madly in love with me. From that place, all my blind spots are now in.

I take responsibility from that place of experiencing Reality madly loving me, madly in love with all of myself, because **a crisis of intimacy means that something is left outside of the circle.**

- That's my blind spot.
- That's me not being madly in love with myself.
- That's me not knowing that Reality is actually, truly, for real, madly in love with me.

Not that I merely *say it*, but the second that I am offscreen or I am doing my private thing, or public thing, all of a sudden I can't find it anymore, and then I act from my blind spot.

I have to live in the known, visceral, experience in my body, *Reality is madly in love with me.* Then, when I act on the stage of my life, whether it's my private stage or my world stage, it doesn't matter. "All of life's a stage," said Shakespeare.

It doesn't matter if it's private or public. I'm going to act in ways that are for the sake of the whole because I'm not trying to fill up my emptiness. Whether I'm a world leader, whether I'm an evolutionary leader, whether I'm a politician, a poet, a bard, a movie star, the head of an NGO, I'm going to act truly, intimately, with the whole. Then it's all going to change.

There's no difference between personal awakening and collective awakening. There is no difference between personal enlightenment and collective enlightenment. Every NGO and every government is part of the solution, because they're part of the problem. Without them, we can't solve the problem.

For the first time in history, we're either going to be genuinely intimate with each other, or we're going to destroy the planet. There's no choice, and we cannot be genuinely intimate with each other unless we are intimate with ourselves.

I am the intimacy that I want to create in the world.

I have to be the intimacy I want to create in the world.

We're modeling to each other what it's like to be madly in love with each other.

> *God, Goddess, give me a sign that you're madly in love with me so that I can have the courage to madly love the world.*

CHAPTER SIX

RESTORE INTIMACY AND BRING POWER BACK INTO THE CIRCLE

Episode 106 — October 27, 2018

EVOLUTIONARY LOVE CODE: CRISIS IS AN EVOLUTIONARY DRIVER

Our crisis is a birth, personally and collectively, because our crisis is an evolutionary driver. Every great crisis is, at its root, a crisis of intimacy. Crisis means that someone or something is being left out of the circle.

In every crisis, ask yourself the question, what's being left out of the circle? The solution to the crisis is a new configuration of intimacy within the circle.

TO BE MADLY IN LOVE WITH MYSELF IS TO KNOW I MATTER INFINITELY

This Evolutionary Love Code applies to every moment of our lives.

Is there anyone that you know that you are ostracizing or leaving out of your circle? Visualize that person, even if you have not talked for years, even if there's been a tremendous fight, even if you don't like or respect this

person. Bring the person into the circle. Judge them not and ask: *What is their heart's desire?* (Both in terms of being left out and coming into the circle or anything, truly be able to comprehend it without judging it.) The more difficult the person, the greater the reward. Feel what happens when you let them into your circle. What happens for them and what happens for you? So, let's dedicate ourselves to this birth—personally, socially, and on a planetary scale.

We're in what I believe is the single most important place on planet Earth, at this moment. I mean that without hyperbole, without exaggeration, without metaphor. The only way we can engage and create a better tomorrow is to create a wave that's larger than any one individual. It's to create a wave of Spirit, a wave of love, a wave of new insight that includes:

- A new Universe Story
- A new narrative of identity
- A new narrative of power
- A new narrative of Eros and relationship
- A new narrative of purpose that every child on the planet grows up knowing

We're at the leading edge. That's a big responsibility. I want us to just get how big this responsibility is. We're the people who are saying, in our bodies, in our personal stories, in our lives, that we're going to *be* the new story. We *are* the new story! We're going to incarnate the new story.

That is not easy. It's not easy to be a little bit ahead of the camp.

I'm going to tell you a little secret. When Jesus was getting crucified, where do you think the important people were? They weren't at the crucifixion. They were in Jerusalem at very important state dinners. They were running webinars. They were doing all sorts of dramatic things. It was only those people *on the side*, they were there at the crucifixion; but the important, serious, mainstream people wouldn't be at that funny event there on the side!

I'll tell you a secret. When it's easy, it gets wildly commodified and becomes a huge business. Blessings to all huge businesses, but that's not the place where the spark of Spirit lives. **The spark of Spirit lives when a band of Outrageous Lovers comes together and says,**

> *You know what? Against all odds. We don't quite have the resources to do it. You know what?* ***We don't even know how it is going to work but we're going to do it.*** *We're going to start. We're going to begin.*

The code says that if something is left out of the circle, we're not intimate. Every crisis is a crisis of intimacy, and we live at this moment of a global intimacy disorder.

It's only by restoring intimacy that we can survive on planet Earth.

We talked last week about climate change being, for the first time in history, a solvable problem which, if we don't solve it, will destroy us. But it's only solvable if every single nation on the planet and every single person is involved. Can you just get the divine joke here?

We're challenged with a global problem which requires solving it through intimacy in which no one is left out. Everyone has an *imprint*. **All of a sudden, my soul print, my Unique Self, has this exterior expression, which is my carbon imprint and my carbon footprint**. I matter, my government matters. There's no one who doesn't matter.

The entire system is interconnected. Our currency system today is completely interconnected. You think it's China and the United States? Our currencies—and currency is money, it's energy—are totally intertwined with each other. There's no separation at all.

You can't even begin to understand policy and the global news without understanding that we're completely enmeshed. Our electric currents, our energies are completely enmeshed. Borders are an illusion.

We can solve the global intimacy disorder only if I have an understanding of myself that *I'm a unique expression of intimacy and desire*, and if I have an understanding of Reality as being *the movement towards ever deeper intimacy*.

What is Evolutionary Church about? Why are we here together? Our external disguise is that we're a church. We run the Center for Integral Wisdom and the Foundation for Conscious Evolution together. Our external disguise is that we're leading-edge think tanks, but that's not who we really are. **We're a band of Outrageous Lovers.**

- ◆ We're committed to loving each other madly!
- ◆ We're committed to liberating love from being just something I say to the person who happens to be living next to me, or my brother or sister, but I forgot what it meant.
- ◆ We're reclaiming Reality's falling in love with itself biologically, atomically, structurally, as allurement in every second.

To paraphrase Meister Eckhart, the great Christian mystic, *Reality can't even stop kissing itself for a moment*. We're here to fall in love. But we're here to fall in love in a particular way, which is, *what have we left out of the circle?*

I want to make a proposition. Here's what we've left out of the circle, leading to our crisis of intimacy. In order to restore intimacy, we have to identify what we've left out of the circle. Last week we talked about leaving out of the circle *being madly in love with myself.* But that brings us to number two.

You see, **when I'm not madly in love with myself, I leave my own power out of the circle—I don't claim my power. I don't get how much I matter.**

We have to sustain, deep inside, that alive sense that we're so in love with Reality, with each other, and with life. I do that only if I realize *I am powerful.*

I (Marc) was talking to someone this week whom I had been writing letters with for about seven years; and I said to this person, who is a dear friend, *friend, don't you realize how powerful you are, that when you stop writing letters, I'm devastated?* Then this person got back to me, *Really? I have an impact in that way?* I said, *of course. Of course!*

We don't get that *we are powerful.* We don't get that we have the *capacity to hurt,* because our words matter. We have the *capacity to heal* because our words matter.

- We are healers of the Cosmos.
- We are Bodhisattvas.
- We are evolutionary mystics.
- We are evolutionary revolutionaries.
- Our words matter.
- We are powerful.

This week what we want to focus on, what we have left out of the circle, is this *knowing that we are powerful.* So, if one of us is hurt, we're devastated. We are willing to be madly in love with each other beyond reason, which means we are willing to feel each other.

TO BECOME LIKE GOD: LOVE MORE

Intimacy is *feel me, feeling you.* We can feel each other all day and all night. **When we feel each other, when we actually feel each other, there will be no climate change.** There will be no issue.

The only reason there's a climate change issue is because part of the world can't feel the other part of the world; we can't feel beyond this moment, and we can't feel our responsibility for a memory of the future.

Let's feel each other, friends. Let's feel each other so beautifully, so *erotically.* But erotically doesn't mean sexually. Sex is beautiful, but that's not what we're about. Erotically means what we would call *supra-sexually.* I use the word Eros meaning we can literally quiver with each other. We can resonate with each other. We can feel each other's joy and feel each other's pain. The greatest ability of a human being in the world is to feel somebody else's holy and broken *Hallelujah*.

Do you know what it means to be God? Feel into this. *I am God*, and by *I*, I don't mean just me; I mean we all are God.

What is God? God is this being. God is not less than a person; God is much more than a person. This is unbelievable. God is this beingness who feels, infinitely deeply, the holy and broken *Hallelujah* of every single person on the planet who ever was, is, or will be.

God is personally, madly in love, passionately desiring every single person and being that is, was, and will be on this planet and within the multiverse, and all other places where there is beingness.

In the same way that you, whoever you are, and I, are madly in love with the person we love most in our lives, so *Goddess* is being madly in love, personally, with every individual beingness that ever was, is, or will be.

If you want to begin to become like God, here's the deal: love more!

If you want to begin to become like God, then your love lists, my love lists, are too short. Expand your love lists! Fall madly in love—more! Not less. That doesn't mean you get a U-Haul and move in with everyone. It means you can hear everybody's broken and holy *Hallelujah*, just like She hears ours.

When we pray, we know that the Infinity of Intimacy that knows our name doesn't leave anybody out of the circle. The reason that the Divine is the Infinity of Intimacy is because no one's out of the circle.

Oh, my Goddess! So, *friends, Romans and countrymen,* as Shakespeare said it, oh my God, beloved Outrageous Lovers, let's pray, and let's model in Reality what it means to put our holy and broken *Hallelujah* before the Divine.

EXERCISE TO OPEN OUR ARMS AND LET THEM ALL IN

Our crisis is a birth. So, let's open the circle and let everybody in. Here's an exercise to start opening the circle with people you might know but really dislike personally. Let's open the circle.

If you can find somebody you have not liked who you have thought has been mean or cruel or lying or cheating or stealing, open the circle, and let them in. See them in the light of the person who is yearning and longing for more love. See them that way. Then open the circle wider and see if we can bring the political situation in.

Let's see if we could bring the Democrats and the Republicans in. Try to feel into those Democrats, those presidential candidates who are giving their lives to try to beat Donald Trump, for good reason. They're all being hit in very difficult ways and then they're trying not to hit back. Let's say that one of them goes up and says, *you know what? As a Democrat, I'm opening my mind, my eyes, and my arms, and I am letting them all in—we're all humans, we're on one planet,* and makes the most gracious, amazing speech where they let go of these divisions that are fabricated in order to win, and instead incorporates the different points of view, all of which have some good to them.

I'm seeing the next level of political leadership. Let's open our arms and let them all in and bring them into the holy *Hallelujah* of the Spirit of Evolutionary Church, the Spirit of Evolutionary Love that's going through everybody, even the worst criminals and culprits of our society.

I'm conjecturing, out of our Holy Church, a holy opening of our arms so wide that, as we are going into that political situation [midterm elections], we have let them all in.

We are playing a role that nobody is fully playing on this planet. It's not just forgiving people. In the end they say, in the New Testament, that forgiveness goes quantum and everything forgives everything else; they can't stop forgiving.

We're at the end times! This means either we go down into catastrophe through climate change and resource depletion and species extinction, or we're going up towards evolution of a new world. We happen to be the culture on the cusp of that.

What hasn't happened yet is any of us having had the power to step out there and open our arms so wide and let everybody in. As we do that, imagine all of those who are outside our global circle being included. *Father forgive them. They know not what they do.*

Feel, as you do this, your power as an Evolutionary Lover. Feel that beautiful phrase, *God needs me.*

- I am needed.
- I am unique.
- I am recognized.
- I am adored.

I'm adored by the God that is the Creator of us all. If we walk out into this planetary system with the power of an agent of planetary evolution, we've crossed over, we're on the other side of the breakdown. We're breaking through. Feel the Church of Evolutionary Love as the place that takes us the next step on the evolutionary spiral.

Can you imagine a way of loving and communicating and experiencing God's love so deeply that we would be able to do what Jesus did when he was crucified? He said, *Father, forgive them, they know not what they do*, as he was killed.

SATURDAY CHURCH IS THE CHURCH OF THE METAMORPHOSIS

Then there was Saturday. Our favorite day in the whole story is Saturday in the tomb of metamorphosis. Nobody really asks, *what happened on Saturday?*

We are a Saturday Church. We really need to acknowledge that. The Saturday Church is the *Church of Metamorphosis*. The crucifixion is what is happening worldwide as people are destroying each other and destroying the planet. In the midst of that, we're here saying, *Father, forgive them, they know not what they do.*

Let's all be in the Saturday Church. **The Saturday Church is the church of the metamorphosis of each other and of humanity toward Sunday, the resurrection from the dead.**

What is that resurrection? When Jesus reappeared and Mary saw him, we know:

- I have the resurrection in my soul.
- I feel the resurrection as a living potentiality in myself and everyone.
- I feel the metamorphosis.

Now, let's jump to the self-organizing Universe. How does the self-organizing universe organize the Universe? It doesn't show up at all—you never see it. There are no big statues to the self-organizing Universe.

What is the self-organizing Universe from the Big Bang, all the way on up through the quarks and the electrons?

The self-organizing Universe is the interior of evolution.

The self-organizing Universe is evolving in this most awesome ability to bring separate parts together to be ever more whole. The Saturday Church is the Church of the Self-organizing Universe.

In the church of the self-organizing Universe, we call upon the self-organizing power that has been able to go from quarks to us, to take us to the next step where we open our arms wide enough to let them all in. All the deplorables, including ourselves. All the deplorables. There are actually no more deplorables. We let them all in.

We are on the other side, and we are dedicating the Evolutionary Church, the church of the Saturday transformation of humanity, to the evolution of love, creativity, and awareness of how the self-organizing universe actually works.

As we bring ourselves ever more closely together, we will understand the resurrection of our culture, by *being that ourselves*. We are given the power, in part through our high technology, used operationally for the metamorphosis of our species from the dying humans to the evolving humanity.

IT'S TIME TO RECLAIM OUR UNIQUE POWER

What's left out of the circle? What's left out is your power, my power. If there's one thing that can change everything, it's the realization that I'm powerful! We're afraid of the word power. We're afraid of it, but we need to reclaim power in the most beautiful and gorgeous sense. Let me retrace the narratives of power throughout history.

- **In the premodern world, before the Renaissance, all the power was with God.** God had all the power, and God was the Infinity of Power, but the human being was emasculated. We couldn't find human power.

- **Along came modernity and said,** *God, you're still invited to the banquet; but really, the power lives in the laws of the universe, that God dumped into the universe; but* **really, the power is with the human being.** But then that human power, that technological explosion, led to the atom bomb. We unleashed a new level of power and we had no story equal to our power.

- **The postmodern world critiqued it and said,** *power is bad!* Foucault came along and said, *power is the most terrible, insidious, horrible human drive.* **So, we were left with no story of power.**

Now, what we need to do is to re-articulate a story of power. Here's the story. Here's the big move. The big move is:

---

*I am powerful because I'm
a personal expression of
Evolutionary Love.*

I am Evolutionary Love, but I'm a unique expression of Evolutionary Love that never was, is, or will be, so I have power to impact.

My words hurt and my words heal. **My words hurt and my words heal because I'm powerful.** I can impact, and I can change, and I can shift. I am power.

What I have left out of the circle of my life is my own power. I'm evolution. I'm uniquely powerful. I'm uniquely powerful beyond measure. Take that sentence on for yourself. Say, *I am power.* Let's first find it in ourselves. Let's just start with, *I am power.* Feel that coursing through you.

THE EVOLUTION OF INTIMACY

Now, let's go to the next step together. The first step is, *I am power*. The second step is, *I am power for,* not just that *I am power over*. Power is not *power over,* power is *power for*. I am power for. Feel it changing you! We think power is just *power over*. Can I find that energy in me which is, *I am power for?*

Now, are you willing to take the next step? Can we go the next step together? Because the next step goes even deeper.

It's not just that I am *power for,* generally. I'm irreplaceable; this is a big deal. I cannot be the power that's someone else's. I can't do it! The power that is, let's say, Terry. You have to get that *Terry is so powerful!* When you decide that you're power and then that you're *unique power for,* then your whole life changes. You wake up in the morning and you ask one question, *what does Reality need from my power?* Because I am Reality's power.

It's, *I'm unique power for,* unlike any other. I'm unique power that never was, is, or will be, and my power has been outside the circle. Reality hasn't felt its own power through me. No one can do what I can do.

Now, this is the fourth and last step. We're doing this together and we're transfiguring. **This is the transfiguration:**

- Reality needs my unique power.
- God needs my unique power.

Whichever word makes it come alive for you—it's the same. Reality and God are the same. Reality, or God, needs my unique power. That's shocking! That's the inner truth of Reality. To get that, my entire life changes.

So, I get up in the morning and I say, *what does evolution, what does Reality, need from me at this moment?* That's the only question we ever need to ask. That is *the* question. The question is not, *to be or not to be?* I am! I am that I am.

*The only question I ask is,
"What does Reality need from
my unique power today?"*

If we just ask that question in the morning, we've claimed our power. Now we're in the same circle. We're in a circle of intimacy, together. Reality needs my unique power. None of us can do it alone. We have to look at each other and say, *just as Reality needs my unique power, Reality needs our unique power*—we are a Unique Self Symphony.

- I first have to realize Reality needs my unique power.
- Then I realize Reality needs your unique power.
- Then I realize Reality needs *our* unique power.

That's not a metaphor. This is not poetry. This is not an exercise. This is the enlightened, democratized consciousness in which I have taken my power back into the circle, because all of us have split off our power.

All of us have split off our power. We don't believe in our power. We speak words that heal and we speak words that hurt. It's only when I don't believe in my unique power that I go to hurt people. I don't get that I have the power of God in me and that God needs my/our unique power.

Here, however, we can look at each other and say:

> We are the revolution. How could anyone ever tell you that you are anything less than beautiful? How could anyone ever tell you that you are less than whole?

Reality needs your and our unique power.

CHAPTER SEVEN

RECLAIMING AND EVOLVING SACRED TEXTS

Episode 107 — November 3, 2018

EVOLUTIONARY LOVE CODE: WHAT IS BEING LEFT OUT OF THE CIRCLE?

Our crisis is a birth, personally and collectively, because our crisis is an evolutionary driver. Every great crisis is, at its root, a crisis of intimacy.

Crisis means that someone or something is being left out of the circle. In every crisis, ask yourself the question, what is being left out of the circle?

The solution to the crisis is a new configuration of intimacy within the circle.

WE WANT A POLITICS OF LOVE AND A LOVE OF POLITICS

Take a moment and place your attention on the crisis in yourself. What's the crisis in yourself? What's being left out? Whatever's being left out, the solution to our crisis is a new configuration of intimacy. Bring what is left out into the circle.

We're at this very painful, gorgeous, excruciating place in world history. We are at this pivotal point in American history. We happen to be just before midterm elections in the United States. They're a very important moment in history. We want to invite something very important here: *a church has to be political.* It's not that church shouldn't be political; a church *is* political. It's always political.

What do we mean when we say, *church is political?* What does that mean? Why do we have a separation of church and state? Separation of church and state is important in one way. The state can't interfere with the church and the church can't legally, structurally, interfere with the free state. That's critical. The separation of church and state is one of the great, momentous leaps in consciousness.

But that doesn't mean that politics isn't about Spirit and that Spirit is not about politics. What is politics about?

- It's about how we live together as a community.
- It's about how we love each other.
- It's about how we take care of each other.

When we talk about, for example, healthcare—that every human being in the world deserves basic healthcare—what we're saying is, *we have to love everybody.* Everyone deserves to be loved. We're saying that we can't have a huge swath of people left out of the social safety net, where a mother in a family gets cancer and the daughter watches her gradually die, because there's no healthcare available for her even though she has worked hard her entire life in order to save money. She was born, perhaps, into a cycle of poverty, was able to raise children, but not able to have enough money to have healthcare. That's actually not okay. It's not okay that someone who is born with a trust fund gets their cancer taken care of, and someone who is not born with a trust fund, who has worked really hard, doesn't get their cancer taken care of.

That's not about politics. That's about love. It's really important to understand.

---

*We want a politics of love, and
we want a love of politics.*

That's absolutely critical.

Now, we have to be really careful in saying and understanding, that there's not the *good guys and the bad guys* here. This is not Democratic politics versus Republican politics. There are a lot of gorgeous, holy Republicans in the world who love people madly.

My colleague Dennis Prager, who has spent his life fighting for ethics, has a deep love for human beings, and he's a major Republican. He runs a radio show in LA. I disagree with a lot of what he says, but he loves people madly, and his entire life is about alleviating suffering.

And there are gorgeous Democrats. We have a good friend who's running for Governor of one of our great states, and he's the heir apparent to Senator Bernie Sanders. We have another friend who's running for Senate in another state as an Independent.

So, this is not about *the bad Republicans and the good Democrats*. This is about politics being an enactment of love.

THE DEMOCRATIZATION OF PRAYER BREAKFASTS

We pray here in church. Prayer Breakfasts,[4] an American political tradition, are not just for fundamentalists—people often think *fundamentalists pray, liberals don't pray.*

---

4 The National Prayer Breakfast is a yearly event held in Washington, D.C., usually on the first Thursday in February, and includes a series of meetings, luncheons, and dinners. It has taken place since 1953.

No, prayer means something in Evolutionary Church. We are reclaiming prayer. Just like the Gospel Church, which was the vehicle for human rights, the Evolutionary Church has to be the vehicle for a planetary awakening in love through Unique Self Symphonies.

The Evolutionary Church *is* the new Gospel Church.

> It's why we sing.
> It's why we *hymn*.
> It's why we pray.

Who are we praying to? We are evolving prayer. We're not praying to the *cosmic vending machine god,* owned by one religion.

The fundamentalists: *Oh, that's our God.* The liberals: *No, that's our God.* Presbyterians: *or is it the God of the Jews?*

No, in fact:

- God is the Infinity of Intimacy that knows your name.
- God is the Infinity of Power.
- God is the incessant, ceaseless creativity of Cosmos that lives in me, as me, and through me, even as God is the She that holds me in every second.

We know this not based on dogma, but based on the interior sciences. When we go deep into the interior face of the Cosmos, we know that just as you hear me speaking right now, so too does the Universe hear me speaking.

Prayer means that the Infinity of Intimacy, the Universe—the one verse that runs through everything—hears every single thing that I say. It's unbelievable! It's shocking!

This week we want to bring together Spirit and politics. We want to bless every candidate who's running for the sake of the evolution of love. This is a politics of Evolutionary Love. What we want to do this week is bring something into the circle.

Here's what we want to bring into the circle. In the code, we said that anything that's left out of the circle creates a crisis of intimacy. The crisis of intimacy, our global intimacy disorder, means that something is not in the circle, something is not *inside*.

> *We create our illusion of being inside the circle by placing someone else outside.*

I'm inside because all the Republicans are bad—they're outside. I'm inside because all the Democrats are bad—they're outside. No! Actually, we all have to be in the circle.

We've also placed something else outside of the circle: **the great, sacred texts of culture.**

- One kind of beautiful, sacred text is the Bill of Rights, and also the Constitution, which are civil sacred texts.
- A second kind of sacred text has been lost. Its true study has been left to fundamentalism, and I'm referring to the great, sacred texts of the scriptures of all the great traditions.

Those scriptures are imperfect. Sometimes they're ethnocentric, sometimes they're homophobic, but underneath the surface structures of those scriptures there's a deep core of resonating intimacy and divinity.

We've left those sacred texts out of the circle. We're not intimate with the sacred texts that need to inform our politics—not in a way that says, *religion runs politics*, but in a way that says, *Spirit and politics are both expressions of love.*

Remember, it's one love. It's one infinity. It's one world, and we need to be talking to each other. We need to be studying sacred texts together. We need to bring sacred texts of Spirit back into the circle. That's what we're going to do.

In this gorgeous Evolutionary Church, which is also a *Revolutionary* Church, right before midterm elections, what we want to say is, *the spiritual is political. And the political is spiritual. There is no split between them.*

Our sacred texts have been left out of the conversation, so the only readings we have are fundamentalist readings. These are readings that say:

- Our God, not your God.
- My way of sexing, not your way of sexing.
- I'm in the circle, and you're outside.

We need to reclaim our sacred texts and give them evolutionary readings. Give them readings that emerge from what we call the evolution of love. That's what we're going to be doing today.

We're doing this with intention for midterm elections. We will read from sacred texts and bring them back in the circle.

Ultimately, these sacred texts allow us to read the ultimate sacred text.

The ultimate sacred text is the sacred text of your heart, the sacred text of my heart.

So, take a moment. Let's come before the Divine and bring our holy and our broken *Hallelujah.*

Literally say, oh my God, Infinity of Intimacy who knows my need, please hear me. Hear me, accept, receive, embrace my holy and broken *Hallelujah.*

This is why we all need to pray.

THE EVOLUTIONARY TESTAMENT: A TEMPLATE FOR THE FUTURE HUMAN

Placing this church in the context of the evolution of humanity, let's go back to see the roots of this church. Let's connect our historical roots with the existing political reality and put our love into it.

Going back to our roots, let's go back to the New Testament. Before we do, I'll just give a little background so we can see how the New Testament paints a picture of the future that we're already bringing in through this church.

I want to share the sequence of influences for how I (Barbara) came to the Evolutionary Testament of co-creation. I came from a Jewish, agnostic, secular, materialistic, and militaristic family, so I got the perfect traditional and modern starting point—and then burst out like a cannonball to where I am today!

First, I was influenced by Maslow. He said, *wellness rather than sickness*, and he had the image of the self-actualizing person who has found chosen work that is intrinsically self-rewarding. So, I became a student of Maslow.

The next one was Teilhard de Chardin, a Catholic Jesuit who never published in his lifetime. Basically, what he saw was that Jesus was the future human. He saw him as the *ultra human*. He saw that the entire direction of evolution, from single cell to multi-cells, from animal to human, was going into what he called the *ultra* human or the Christ.

Sri Aurobindo called it the *gnostic* human.

Buckminster Fuller called it the *continuous* human. All my future-oriented guides were able to offer this.

Then I met some Catholic sisters, who are really running the church. They are absolutely great. They almost made me into a Catholic sister. They kept saying to me, *when did you become a Catholic, Barbara?* And I said, *well, I'm not a Catholic. Well,* they said, *you certainly sound like one*! They had been influenced by Brian Swimme, and they'd been deeply influenced by the evolutionary philosophy of Pierre Teilhard de Chardin and other great thinkers.

They invited me to speak before all the Catholic women of the world who are running the church. I spoke on conscious evolution. An article was written in a key Catholic newspaper saying that a woman had come to be a speaker at the Catholic Sisters to arrange a global convening. The article said, *this woman dared to talk about "conscious evolution."* And they were afraid that it would destroy the faith of the sisters.

The Vatican also thought that conscious evolution would destroy the faith of the Catholic sisters. So, the Catholic sisters made me, along with the feminists, who were also loathed, into their "worst of all"—a woman who was a *conscious evolutionary*.

One day, taking a walk, I (Barbara) saw a huge statue of the resurrection there in the garden in Santa Barbara and the inner voice said:

> *Barbara, when you love God above all else, when you love your neighbor as yourself, and when you love yourself as a natural Christ, combined with science and technology, you will all be changed. I want demonstrations now, Barbara. I want you to be a demonstration of the love of God, of nature, of Self as a natural Christ, aided and abetted by science and technology, giving us the power of gods.*

The awesome reality is that is exactly what's coming.

I'm setting out a huge path here for the Evolutionary Church, which is to go back to the ancient texts, and the history they've created on this Earth, and then jump forward into the very growing edge of our culture.

Let's bring this in, and let's reunite all those other churches who believe in this. Let's invite them to join with us in seeing what's becoming, what's emerging. This is a huge thing.

Let's look at two small gospels out of *The Evolutionary Testament of Co-Creation.*[5]

From Matthew Chapter 1, verses 1–3; the Gospel according to Matthew:

> In those days came John the Baptist, preaching in the wilderness of Judea, and saying, *repent all of you: for the Kingdom of Heaven is at hand. For this is He that was spoken of by the prophet Isaiah, saying, the voice of one crying in the wilderness. Prepare, all of you, the way of the Lord. May his path be made straight.*

This is my interpretation: An intuition lives deep in the memory of humankind informing us that we're more than animals destined to repeat the endless mammalian cycle of eating, sleeping, reproducing, and dying. That's the mammalian cycle!

The words of John the Baptist reveal to us that we're unfinished. Something more awaits us: the release of our potential, a fulfillment of our aspiration.

Repent, John said, *for the Kingdom of Heaven is at hand.* Repent means to change our minds, to be dissatisfied with our present, incomplete condition, knowing that within us is a state of being much greater than we have yet realized. We are the Kingdom of Heaven when our full potential is realized. Say I, *Repent! Transform! Align with God. Do not accept your present limits. The time for newness is at hand.* Now is that true, folks? The newness is at hand!

Here's Matthew Chapter 3, verses 9 and 10.

> And think not to say, within yourselves, we have Abraham to our father. For I say unto you, that God is able of these stones, to raise up children unto Abraham. And now, also the axe is laid unto the root of the trees. Therefore, every tree which brings not forth good fruit is hewn down and cast into the fire.

---

5   Barbara Marx Hubbard, *The Evolutionary Testament of Co-Creation: The Promise Will Be Kept* (2015).

This is what was said by John the Baptist, who prepared the way for Jesus, and told the Jews, the sons of Abraham, that they would be known by their acts, not by their lineage.

Any act that does not serve the good will be unable to take root and thrive in the new world.

Only the good will endure. It does not matter where we come from or where our parents are, it matters only who we are, where we're going and whether or not we will deliver our highest potential.

Just try to imagine that world with someone preparing the way for that new human that we find ourselves becoming, just now. That new human appears as Jesus. I'll just read you this:

> Then comes Jesus from Galilee to Jordan, unto John to be baptized of him. But John forbade him saying, *I have need to be baptized by you. Come you to me.*

> And Jesus answered, said unto him, *Suffer it to be so now. For thus it becomes us to fulfill all righteousness.*

Let's realize that what we have here is the root of Western culture and, to some degree, the root of all world-oriented evolutionary culture: a being who came in and manifested what we're now becoming.

I (Barbara) was astonished by something while reading and writing this book, which was the same time that I was friends with Jonas Salk, who was taking me to these laboratories where they would say phrases like *stamp out physical death!* Then I had read in the New Testament that Jesus said, *Lazarus arise!* And Lazarus arose. *You shall not die.*

So, I thought, Western culture, and modern culture in general, is developing capacities to act out the vision of life ever evolving. Our New Testament was the first enormous writing from this person who knew all this.

The next passage, which I mentioned in another book of mine called *The Revelation*,[6] comes from Corinthians 15:51–53. St. Paul wrote:

> Behold, I show you a mystery: We shall not all sleep; but we shall all be changed in a moment, in the twinkling of an eye, at the last trumpet. For the trumpet shall sound, and the dead shall be raised incorruptible, and we shall all be changed.

Is it possible that the church of Evolutionary Love is actually the site for the church of the evolving human? That by bringing these ancient texts, as well as the highest degree of current knowledge, into our church we will set a template for the future of humanity as an Evolutionary Church?

INTEGRATING THE DEPTH STRUCTURES OF EVERY GREAT TRADITION

Our code says that *every great crisis is, at its root, a crisis of intimacy.* A crisis means that someone or something is being left out of the circle. This week we're saying: **What we have left out of the circle are our sacred texts that need to inform our politics.** That's a surprising thing to say. After all, aren't we the progressive people? Are we making a fundamentalist claim that the Prayer Breakfast should define policy?

Yes, the Prayer Breakfast should define policy! Yes, we're saying something shocking. But it shouldn't just be the Prayer Breakfast of a regressive fundamentalism. We have to loosen the grip of a fundamentalist reading on these texts and reclaim these texts at a higher level of consciousness. This is so deep.

What is a sacred text?

---

6   Barbara Marx Hubbard, *The Revelation: A Message of Hope for the New Millennium* (1995).

A sacred text is a moment in time in which Spirit downloaded into humanity.

Human spirit went into the interior face of Cosmos and had a realization, or a set of realizations, about the nature of Reality itself, and wrote it down. Wow! There are different sacred texts all over the world, my friends. The sacred texts themselves said two kinds of things. I (Marc) wrote some of this in my afterword to the gorgeous *Evolutionary Testament,* and some of it I wrote in *Radical Kabbalah,* these two volumes on sacred texts. But this is so gorgeous, my friends. Let's open our hearts! Let's actually fix the source code together.

In sacred texts there were two kinds of information. One kind of information is what we're going to call *depth structures.* Depth structures means the deepest reading of the nature of Reality. The wild story is that in all the sacred texts around the world, which we have just been able to gather and really, deeply compare in the last one hundred and fifty, two hundred years, it turns out that **there are about ten major depth structures of what I call the interior sciences.**

The sacred texts reveal the interior sciences. On about ten major issues, all of the sacred texts agree. So that's not dogma. Do you get it?

There's a second part in sacred texts where we get confused. That's why we left them aside. The second part of information in sacred texts is *dogma.*

Dogma is the surface, not the depth, of a sacred text.

The dogma is the part that says, *we are the chosen people and you are not.* The dogma says, *if you don't do this, you may be burned at the stake.*

- ◆ That's dogma.
- ◆ That's cultural triumphalism.

- That's the ethnocentric moment.
- Those parts of the sacred text come through broken prisms of culture and history.

We need to let the dogma go because what unites us is so much greater than what divides us.

Then we need to go back to the sacred texts and identify their deepest structures. The deepest shared depth of sacred texts comes from doing the deepest experiments in meditation and introspection, and from the most beautiful, shared revelations from around the world. **All the sacred texts from around the world agree on the ten most important principles of Reality.** It's shocking because they weren't talking to each other. They didn't know each other, and yet, in this double-blind experiment—once we gather the results of these experiments from all over the world—it turns out that there are ten major principles of Reality that the sacred texts agree on. **That's what we need to reclaim.**

So, it's the *Qu'ran* in its deepest, most evolved form. It's the New Testament in its deepest, most evolved form. I want to just go in deeply with you.

What's the basic realization of sacred text? What is its deepest knowing? Below are some of the principles of this deepest knowing, the deepest realization, of sacred texts:

The deepest knowing of sacred text is:

- First, **Spirit is real.** Inside this material world there is this deep interior. This deep interior is alive. It's the revelation of the sound of music. Remember that movie from way back when? *The hills are alive.* It is all alive. All the way up and all the way down. Sentience, we would call it. Living Reality, all the way up and all the way down. Nothing is dead. There's no inert matter. There's aliveness!
- Second, aliveness is good. **Aliveness seeks the goodness, truth and beauty of Reality.** That's the second great

99

realization of sacred text.

- The third realization of sacred text is, **we fall away from aliveness. We get lost.** That is always the story of the fall, the Garden of Eden. You get exiled from the garden. Every sacred text begins with some version of a fall. The third realization of sacred text is: we always fall away.

- The fourth realization of sacred text, all the sacred texts integrated into one, is: there's a road back. **After your fall, there's a road back.**

- Five, **the road back is through practice.** You can practice deeply and profoundly, and, in that gorgeous practice, you can find your way back.

- Six, and **when you find your way back after falling**, you find your way back to truth, to enlightenment, to awakening, to Spirit, **you are deeper, more alive, more energized, more delighted, more sacred, more good, more true, and beautiful than before the fall.**

- Seven, and then you wake up as love in action. **You become the God-force yourself.** You reach out to the person next to you to heal and transform Reality.

That's what the sacred text says. It says it in many different languages, in many different ways, but here is the thing: We need to do two things now, and this is the program of Evolutionary Church. We need to, as Barbara says so beautifully, recover the old, sacred texts and read them more deeply. It can't be that prayer breakfasts are owned by the far right. Prayer breakfasts are something we all do.

We are reclaiming prayer at a higher level of consciousness. It can't be that Bible reading is owned by a particular party.

We all have to be reading the Qu'ran and the Bible, and reading them carefully.

WE ARE THE ONES TO WRITE THE NEW SACRED TEXTS

I want to invite you to join a synagogue, join a church, join a mosque, be part of an organized religion, for sure—and—we have to do something else.

We have to write a new sacred text.
There have to be new sacred texts.

What we're trying to do in the Great Library, at The Foundation for Conscious Evolution and the Center for Integral Wisdom, is to write a new set of sacred texts.

We have to integrate together the deepest truths of all the sacred texts of the great traditions, as well as the deepest truths of modernity, which are the sciences like the schools of psychology. We have to integrate the great, ancient sacred texts that are the truths of the traditional period until the Renaissance, then all the best truths of modernity, the best truths of evolution. We have to take all of those and integrate them together. We have to write new sacred texts.

I want to feel into this together. Here is the sentence. **We're the ones to write the new sacred texts. We are the ones! That's what the Great Library is.** It's bigger than anything else. It's the Cosmic Syncon.[7] We're doing the Cosmic Syncon. We're the ones to write the new sacred texts; it is us!

To write a new sacred text, we can't just make it up. We can't just say things. We have to study the sacred texts, to commit ourselves. Barbara has been writing in her journal for decades, every morning. I (Marc) have spent the last year trying to write new sacred texts. I have written, this is not an exaggeration, about eight hundred thousand words, over ten volumes. We are committing all of our lives, together with you, with all of us together, to write the new sacred texts. We're the ones to write the new sacred texts.

---

7 Shorthand for "synergistic convergence," a model of cooperation and social action.

Writing the new texts is radical dedication, radical commitment, and radical joy.

I want to tell you a holy, crazy secret. There's no greater joy than to write a new sacred text. Here's the story, and it's so radical. It comes from radical dedication and radical commitment. Feel how Barbara's words in the Evolutionary Testament above, and my words from *Radical Kabbalah* resonate together, because it's the word of sacred text. It is one. It's so gorgeous.

Here's a text from the nineteenth century from Franz Kafka's Hasidic master, named Nachman of Breslov. How do you write a new sacred text? Nachman of Breslov says, *by the rivers of Babylon, there we sat and there we wept*—which is the text of the prophet. He says, *By the rivers of Babylon*. What that means is, when you sit in Babylon, you sit in exile. He says, *you have to first cry*. If you can first cry, and purify yourself with tears, you can then write sacred texts. He's referring to what's called the *Babylonian Talmud*.

The great Talmud is the great word of God, a sacred text written in the Hebrew tradition. He says, *by the rivers of Babylon, there we sat, there we wept*. He says that the way you write the Babylonian Talmud is to first cry.

- We have to write our new Talmud, a global, transnational Talmud, our new sacred text. But to do it, we have to cry first.
- We have to go into our loneliness.
- We have to go into our brokenness.
- We have to go into our holy and our broken *Hallelujah*.
- We have to write from the deepest realization that comes from our joy and our ecstasy and from our brokenness.
- We have to write from our deepest life experience, but not to

cover up the emptiness. Knowing that every tear is precious. Knowing that all laughter is filled with revelation.

We can write sacred texts only when we know that we're the ones, only when we're madly in love with ourselves, when we're willing to sacrifice ourselves. It's not *my* sacred text—*Oh let me write my original new idea today*. No, we're all writing it together.

We're all the sacred texts together.

We're all trying to create the sacred text together. Just feel that.

You have to be willing to cry, and you have to be willing to laugh.

You have to be willing to go into the deepest place.

You have to be willing to sit with the insecurity and to be in that deep, radical devotion.

We are the ones.

CHAPTER EIGHT

I AM LOVE IN ACTION: INTIMACY, CREATIVITY, AND THE NEW HUMAN

Episode 108 — November 10, 2018

EVOLUTIONARY LOVE CODE: EACH CRISIS OF INTIMACY IS A BIRTH

Our crisis is a birth, personally and collectively, because our crisis is an evolutionary driver.

Every great crisis is, at its root, a crisis of intimacy.

Crisis means that someone or something is left out. In every crisis, ask yourself the question, what's being left out of the circle?

The solution to the crisis is a new configuration of intimacy within the circle.

THE ONLY DECISION IS TO OPEN MY HEART

We can hold this crisis of intimacy in our hearts, as what's often being left out is our own deepest selves. Not just someone or something else, but the essence of ourselves as new humans.

Let's go back to the pilgrims, for a moment. Remember the pilgrims? It's a great Christian tradition, of course, which starts in the Hebrew tradition. The pilgrims would go to Jerusalem. They would go three times a year and they would go to see God's face.

What is God's face? God's face is when you step out of your routine, and you step into the deep, true essence of Reality itself. You're blown out of your mind. You're like, o*h my God, this is what Reality is!* That's what *seeing God's face* was. That's what Jerusalem was.

Jerusalem, as we have said, is *whole consciousness.* Jerusalem is *yirah*, which means *awe, awesome,* and *shalem,* awe, awesome, or *salem or shalom*, the same word, the full experience of awesomeness. That's what the word Jerusalem means. Jerusalem means the full experience of awesomeness.

What they did was a pilgrimage. Pilgrimage in Hebrew is *aliyah,* which means to go up, and *laregel,* by foot. But if we play in Hebrew for a second, the word *regel,* which means foot, going up by foot, also means *regular.* Regular, meaning, *I go up from the regular*, means I transcend my routine, and I have this immersion in total awesomeness.

That's what Evolutionary Church is. The vision of Evolutionary Church is that it will ultimately become a place on the planet where a person can come once a week and do a complete reset and re-access the truth of their being. That is the practice we're talking about.

I've articulated seven basic principles of Reality that are shared by all the great traditions. One of the principles is you always fall away. You always do. You never *not* fall away—everybody does. Anyone who tells you they never fall away is psychotic.

Everybody falls away.

That's the nature of Reality: we open and close. So, in order to reopen, I open.

The only decision we ever make in life is this: are we open or closed?

- You can be in the middle of giving a great speech and have everyone being blown out of their mind—and you're closed.
- You can be in the middle of an orgasm and be closed.
- Or you can be walking down the street simply to take your child to kindergarten and have your heart totally open.
- When you're open, Reality opens.

How do you open? **You open when you access the truth of what's real**. That's what Evolutionary Church is. We step in, and it's better than being in a physical church. In a physical church there are a million distractions. Now, we miss being physically together, that is true, but here we have a total immersive experience. Our commitment is to up-level church. We are going to up-level it because we're going to get deeper. We will up-level the technology, but our biggest up-level is our internal technology. We're always up-leveling the technology of our hearts.

To up-level our technology, my friends, we have to up-level our hearts. We have to open our hearts wider and wider.

Just imagine this for one second: virtual reality. Virtual reality is the wave of the future, but what is virtual reality? It is the *Jerusalem experience* exponentialized. Instead of going up to Jerusalem, we can now gather in the nervous system of the planet, on the web, and we can have a virtual experience where we are totally focused. Then we go inside.

I want to add something about the first two principles that all the sacred texts share:

The first principle is, Spirit is alive. Spirit is real, and realness is alive. It's *aliveness all the way up and all the way down*. Sentience, all the way up and all the way down. *The hills are alive with the sound of music.* It's all alive; everything is alive.

The second principle is that in order to find it, you have to go inside. To find it, to access it, you have to go inside. When you go inside, that's where you find it. Once you go inside, then you step out of the inside, you look everywhere, and you realize that *everything* is inside. As Lao Tzu was getting at, *there is no inside, there is no outside—it's all alive.* You have to go inside—that's what church is. **We go inside to this immersive experience of Outrageous Love, together. That's how we become the new human and the new humanity.**

We're going to invoke the new human, we're going to invoke the new humanity, because that's what we're about. The Church of Evolutionary Love is the place of the invocation of the new human and the new humanity.

The new human is *Homo amor universalis*: the human being who's a unique expression of Evolutionary Love, who's the leading edge of evolution as love in action.

We are not just here for ourselves. We are totally here for ourselves, we're madly in love with ourselves, and we understand that our self is part of the larger Self. That's our center of gravity: that the only response to the crisis of intimacy is to become intimate with our True Self.

Our True Self is our Unique Self, our Evolutionary Unique Self, our future self calling us forward. We have to incarnate what it means to be madly in love with each other, to be madly in love with life, and to open our hearts again and again.

We have to go inside in this immersive experience and let it flow into the week, so we become expressions, incarnations, Outrageous Evolutionary Lovers acting as love in action, as part of a Unique Self Symphony which rises—all boats rise together.

It's about being together once a week. It's about coming together and contributing to create an Evolutionary Church that becomes a tidal wave of Outrageous Love, a tidal wave of conscious evolution, a tidal wave of Evolutionary Love that sweeps Reality.

That is what we often say: that is what da Vinci and his friends did in modernity. They told the story. They invoked the new human and the new humanity. Evolutionary Church is the ambassador of the new human and the new humanity. To do that, we go inside and immerse. We immerse in the virtual, in this virtual reality, and virtue explodes with delight!

In order to do that there's no bypass road. Since there's no bypass road, we have to bring everything before God. When we say *God,* what do we mean? We don't mean Santa Claus. We don't mean the old man or woman in the sky.

When we say God, we mean the Infinity of Intimacy.

GENUINE CREATIVITY COMES FROM INTIMACY WITH MYSELF

Here is a principle of intimacy. Intimacy is a big principle, a new principle; this is a huge principle. Are you ready? **Intimacy is creative.** We're adding this to the principles of intimacy. Intimacy is creative. It's a huge principle. **Creativity is a byproduct, an expression of intimacy.** Barbara and I (Marc) come together and say, *let's be whole mates,* which is about intimacy. From that intimacy comes creativity!

It's *joining genius,* which is an intimate act. It's intimacy that creates creativity. Creativity is a subset of intimacy. In the virtuous loop between them, creativity then, in turn, creates intimacy. Do you see how gorgeous that is?

- A subset of Eros is intimacy.
- Eros, in part, means interconnected.
- The inside of interconnectivity is intimacy.
- Intimacy generates creativity.

- Creativity itself then generates more intimacy.

So, when we turn to the Divine, to God, we're turning to the Infinity of Intimacy who's also the source of all creativity because infinity generates intimacy. Divine intimacy has to generate creativity.

Those great thinkers who all said God had, as it were, *no choice* but to create the world, what they really meant to say is this: **because Divinity is the Infinity of Intimacy, intimacy *has to* generate creativity.** It can't not.

I'm going to tell you something very deep. When people break intimacy, even though they can do a great creative project, it's actually non-intimate. Intimacy means friendship, and it means depths and it means loyalty and it means authenticity. It's not capitalist; it's not about making deals. This is a very big deal.

---

*If I bypass intimacy in myself
and with myself, I can't be
genuinely creative.*

So, what we do is turn to the Divine, to God, who is the Infinity of Intimacy, who knows our name, who is the source of all creativity and we say,

Oh my God, I'm an expression of You. I'm Homo amor universalis. I'm a unique configuration of intimacy, and I participate in You. I am part of You. You are my lover. You are part of me.

We turn to the Divine and say:

- You are my lover!
- Can I tell You everything that just happened to me last night?
- Can I share with You how lonely I was yesterday?
- Can I share with You how ecstatic I was?

Sometimes we're afraid to go all the way, but with the Infinity of Intimacy we can go all the way. Remember when you were in the shower and you had the showerhead and you were doing a full concert on microphone, and you were singing all the arias? I love to sing in the shower!

You can go all the way to your holy *Hallelujah* where you can be greater than great. God's not going to be jealous; that's the great thing about the Divine. And I share all my brokenness. I bring it all, my *holy and my broken Hallelujah*.

I'm radically intimate with myself: nothing is left out of the circle. We're radically intimate with each other. If there's one thing we do in Evolutionary Church it's that we open our hearts and we unabashedly fall madly in love with ourselves, with each other, and with the Infinity of Intimacy.

We bring our holy and our broken *Hallelujah*; we contemplate the hymn of Leonard Cohen. We offer our prayers. What we're doing is we're weaving the source code. Wow!

Principle two of these seven great principles is that: you have to go inside. Spirit is real. I go inside. How do I go inside? One major way is we hang out in Evolutionary Church, we create a virtual reality, an immersive experience in the Infinity of Intimacy.

WHAT IS BEING LEFT OUT IS OUR NEWNESS

I (Barbara) am a frequent writer in my journal. It's been such a power for me. I am on journal number 204. It started when I was eighteen years old and I wrote just about every day. I had two ways of writing. One was the mental: here's what's going on, here's what I am dealing with. Then, the other was the deeper self, which is not only prayer, but the deep knowing that's in everybody about what's going on if you allow the mental mind to be quiet and you **tap into the mind that's the expression of the deepest impulse of creation in every one of us**.

Through writing, we bring that deepest impulse of creation up to consciousness, not only as my prayers but also what the deeper self knows. The deeper self won't fully inform me unless I *truly* ask. *Ask and it is given; knock and doors are opened.*

There's so much meaning in prayer and in the written word and in allowing yourself to write from deep self. I pray for 100 percent intimacy. Ive been thinking a lot about intimacy in the past few days and I realized that:

> ## *To the degree I can be 100 percent intimate is the degree to which I can be 100 percent revealed as who I am, and who It is, who the world is.*

Out of going the whole way with being intimate with our beloveds, comes the newness and the birth of who we truly are.

Apply that to the particular code of today: *Our crisis is a birth. Crisis is an evolutionary driver.* The crisis means that something is being left out. Here is the insight I had about what's being left out.

Let's place and feel ourselves now in the crisis not only of our own lives but the crisis of the birth of a new culture, the crisis of the breakdown of the old, and the breakthrough of the new, the crisis of climate change, and the possible devolution of our species.

I don't think it's any accident that our church was formed during the crisis of the birth of humanity in which none of the existing structures have a way of communicating. The great churches with the great texts of the past had hints of the new, but they projected it into another realm altogether, whereas here we are—the new!

What's being left out in our own personal crisis of birth, right now? **It could well be that what's being left out of our crisis of birth is the birth of the**

new human as ourselves. In other words, if you really feel that you're an emerging human, then in that sense you're new. You're not your typical, daily person. What's new about you is very often left out when you feel you're in crisis.

When you're able to reconnect with what's genuinely emergent in you, you're at the same time connecting with the impulse of evolution itself as you. In other words, what's emerging is you as an expression of the impulse of creation, of universal evolution. That's who you are.

If you've left yourself out of the experience of yourself being new, you're leaving *yourself being new* outside of the circle—you're not intimate with yourself.

I just had a brief flash of what it feels like to be a fertilized egg. We can't probably remember that, but it was explosive. It was really explosive. The first thing that happens with that little, tiny, fertilized egg when the sperm enters the egg is the heart. A little heartbeat turns on in that little, tiny zygote and, as you know, it goes all the way through the history of development, and it comes out as a new baby.

I'm going to say that we, in our generation, could be considered like a cultural baby born through the womb of evolution into the new human, the new church, and the new potentiality of humanity all together.

We are yet to fully experience what it would be like to live through the intimacy of our union with that deeper self, which is what we've been calling *Homo amor universalis*. Maybe what's been left out of so many of us is the actual experience of our newness.

Let's feel into *Homo amor universalis* as what's being left out in the crisis of birth, and let's see if we can have a feeling of intimacy with the newness that we are. I'll just make an effort to do that for myself, and let's do it for ourselves. **You want to be intimate in the crisis of the birth of yourself, which then leads to the birth of everybody else that you're connected with, and of the world.**

Let's just take it personally first. In order to stay in touch with yourself during your emergence as a new human, it requires a very deep attention on the experience of that inner impulse of evolution that came from the quarks, the electrons, the protons, and neutrons all the way through the genius of evolution, all the way up to where the new human is being born among *Homo sapiens* all over this planet.

I believe new humans are coming forward out of *Homo sapiens*, like us. It's not that we're all great geniuses of the old kind; we're geniuses of the new kind. What's the new kind of genius? **We're this new kind of genius of accessing the uniqueness of ourselves and sharing our genius with each other**, joining genius in supra-sexual co-creation toward a world equal to our potential.

What I would like us to consider here is that the church is the birthing place of this new human. I would like to invite each of us to feel right now that we're giving birth to that new human within ourselves. Let's take some time to just experience anything new that's being born as you.

When I consider what's new being born in me, I have faith in the birth. What is new that's being born in *you* that might have been left out of your feeling of being the human that you are becoming? Because if we're becoming, we are new!

I AM LOVE IN ACTION

We're love in action. We're the leading edge of evolution, and evolution itself is love in action. Evolution itself is intimacy in action. These are the core codes of our church. We've been working on articulating these codes, and we're creating a new Great Library together.

We're coming together and understanding in ourselves that:

We are evolution. Evolution is not out there—evolution is in here.

By *in here*, I point to my chest, my heart, our heart, the One Heart.

- ◆ That's not a sweet idea.
- ◆ It's not a metaphor.
- ◆ It's not a spiritual idea.

I'm anti-spiritual. I don't like spirituality because spirituality is Spirit removed from life, as in, *there's this real life—and then there's Spirit.*

No, the best leading edge of science, exterior science and interior science, leads us to understand that what drives evolution itself is the allurement to deeper and higher intimacies. Evolution is about the evolution of intimacy, the evolution of love.

There is one question we all ask ourselves: *Do you want to play a larger game? Do you want to participate in the evolution of love?* That's our question, and our answer in the church is a resounding, *Yes!* The church *is* the evolution of love. That's what we are. It is a church, and it is a synagogue, it is a mosque, and it is a secular center. It's bigger than anything. **We are, each of us, the leading edge of the evolution of love.**

Let's just first feel our *Yes!* Our evolutionary *Yes,* our holy *Yes.* Let's let all of Reality say *Yes!* In the original Hebrew, the word *Yes* is *kein. Kein* means integrity. My integrity is in my *Yes.*

The next step is to get, profoundly and deeply, that *I am love in action.* That is who I am. Who am I? I am love in action. That's not extra. That's not extraneous to my identity.

Let's take it the next step. To really get this, my whole life changes. This is the interior truth of Reality validated by all the interior sciences: **my love is needed by all of Reality.** My love! My love is needed not just by my one partner, or friend. Can I actually get that my love is needed? That is an ontological fact. That's what we know in systems theory. It's what we know in general dynamics theory. It is what we know in the interior sciences.

My love is, ontologically, *for realsies*, needed by all of Reality. **If I don't give my love to all of Reality, it means there's a part of the world that remains unloved.**

A part of the world remains unloved if I don't stand on the abyss of darkness and say, *Let there be light.* There's a unique configuration of light which is the configuration of intimacy that's me because—*who am I?*—I am a unique configuration of intimacy and desire needed, adored, recognized, intended, chosen by all of Reality. That's who I am.

The *dharma* can't just be self-help. The *dharma* has to be the ontology, the true, real nature of Reality.

If you put a .357 Magnum to my head, if you were Clint Eastwood and you said, *make my day*, and gave me one hour to tell you, for real, the true goal of all of the Evolutionary Love Codes and all of the Great Library and all of Evolutionary Church I would say, *the reification of love.* Clint Eastwood would probably ask, *what's the reification of love?* and then kill me, so by reification I mean, *to understand that love is real.*

Reification means that love is the quality of the center of Reality. But it's not ordinary love. It is not a Harlequin romance. Those are glimmers, fractal glimmers, of that which is most real.

Love is real means integrity matters.

Love is real means that if you can get away with doing a deal, and you can get away with pulling it off, but it's not true, then you're in violation.

Love is real is the power of love. **Abuse means you use your power to violate intimacy.** That's what abuse is. You use your power to violate intimacy, whether that's violating integrity, or loyalty, or the truths of what is.

Remember, in Jerusalem when Jesus was getting crucified, all the New Age leaders were in Jerusalem sending out mailings—I promise! There were like nine people out there by the crucifixion, but everyone else wanted to show up at what they thought were the big events in Jerusalem. *We don't want to miss the big event because I won't be part of it!* They were there sending out mailings and they were doing stuff and poor Jesus was there being crucified with Mary Magdalene and a couple of friends.

But actually, none of the big events and none of the mailings matter.

You know why? Because at that event, at that crucifixion, there was intimacy. It was true intimacy. There was loyalty. There was integrity, and there was a vision beyond the moment. There was a vision beyond the commodification of Spirit. I could say this in a Buddhist way, and I could say it in a secular humanist way and I could say it in a Jewish way and now I happen to be choosing a Christian way. Jesus brought before the Father his holy and his broken *Hallelujah.* Jesus said two things on the cross.

He said, *forgive them, Father, for they know not what they do.* That was his holy *Hallelujah.*

Then he said, *Eli, Eli lama azavtani, God, my God, why have you forsaken me?* That's the holy and the broken *Hallelujah.*

We're ripped apart in pain. We're ripped open in pain, and that pain turns into sweetness and into love and into outrageous intimacy.

- All of us get hurt.
- All of us get betrayed. We only get betrayed by people who could never betray us.
- We've all betrayed.
- We've all not kept a promise we wanted to keep in the world.
- We've all fallen because we all fall away from Spirit.

That's part of the core principles. And then we find our way back again. We open our hearts again. My love is needed by all of Reality. Reality needs me to open my heart again. I am love in action. The Church of Evolutionary Love is where we come together as the Unique Self Symphony, and we realize evolution is the evolution of intimacy.

Evolution desires intimacy. Evolution wants intimacy.

Intimacy means *shared identity*. We are part of the same identity; shared identity, that's beautiful!

Intimacy means *mutuality of recognition,* but recognition doesn't mean just that we see each other—I can see you.

It means I can also feel you. I feel me feeling you, feel you feeling me. I recognize, it's a *mutuality of feeling.* It's a mutuality of pathos. We recognize, we see each other, and we feel each other.

Intimacy is *mutuality of a great purpose.* We join genius. We come together intimately because intimacy births creativity. We have a shared purpose.

We're looking at the horizon together.

CHAPTER NINE

TRANSFORMATION THROUGH EVOLVING THE CAPACITY FOR INTIMACY

Episode 109 — November 17, 2018

EVOLUTIONARY LOVE CODE: THE HIGHEST TRANSFORMATION

Reality is driven by pleasure. The highest pleasure is transformation. Every human being is born to effect a unique personal transformation.

Every human being is born to effect a unique social transformation. Wisdom is knowing what is yours to transform and what is not.

The highest transformation is the transformation of everything.

The highest knowing is to know that your radical commitment to your unique transformation is what transforms everything.

WHEN I OPEN MY HEART, I OPEN THE HEART OF REALITY

Every time in history when we stood between dystopia and utopia, between destruction, pain, and

suffering and the possibility to up-level our consciousness, to participate in the evolution of love, what always happened was a group of people came together, and they said:

- We're going to stand for the evolution of love.
- We're going to stand for the evolution of intimacy.
- We're going to stand together.

What matters more than anything else in Evolutionary Love is that we love each other madly. How we love each other, how we open our hearts in all the private and the public moments, that's who we are.

But we're not just opening our hearts because we want to just feel good for a second. We're opening our hearts because we want to open the heart of Reality. We know, *when I open my heart, I open the heart of Reality*. That's what we are going to be talking about today. We're going to be talking about what that means and how it is that opening my heart opens the heart of all of Reality.

As stated above, every moment in history when we're facing crisis—and a crisis is always a crisis of intimacy—the response to the crisis is a new configuration of intimacy. It's always what happens. We come together. A new configuration of intimacy is always *shared identity*.

With all due respect to the New Age, intimacy is not "into me you see." There's a dimension of that in intimacy, but intimacy, at its core, is shared identity.

The evolution of intimacy is the evolution of shared identity.

As I move and expand my circles of felt love from my immediate circle to my tribe, to every human being on the planet, to Reality itself, I'm participating in the evolution of love, which is the evolution of intimacy.

Let's pray. We're praying to evolve prayer. We're turning to God to participate, as God, in the evolution of God. When we talk about God in Evolutionary Church we're trying to reset, we're trying to *hack God*, as it were. We want to reset what we mean by God.

We don't just mean the ethnocentric, homophobic cosmic vending-machine god in the sky.

We also don't mean the kind of human potential movement claiming, *oh, God is just within; I am God.* Whoa! Easy on the *I am God,* guys.

We're talking about a more nuanced, beautiful, holy, stunning, awesome vision in which we understand that **Divinity is love in action, the third person of the Divine, which is the inherent ceaseless creativity of Cosmos**, *tat tvam asi,* Thou Art That, the unique expression of LoveIntelligence that lives in me, as me, and through me.

In prayer we turn to Divinity in her second person, as *She,* as when Rumi talked about falling into the arms of the Beloved. We think of Divinity, and we feel Divinity, not merely as the Infinity of Power, but as the Infinity of Intimacy.

Let's just feel that in our bodies. Before I ever understand an idea, I *feel* an idea. Let's just feel it. What does it mean? Imagine—let's just meditate together. Think about your most intimate moment, your most tender, intimate, alive, sensual, delighted moment. It might be with a beloved, with a son, a daughter, a friend. Whoever it was with, recall your most intimate moment—*exponentialized!*

Then begin to feel into what it means to know that the Infinity of Intimacy that knows your name feels like that towards you—*exponentialized!* We think about exponential tech, so let's think about exponential intimacy.

So we turn to the Infinity of Intimacy that knows our name, and we say we want to bring everything before You. Everything. Let's consider the complexity, the details, the wonder, the agony, the ecstasy of our lives, our holy and our broken *Hallelujah.*

This is a church, a synagogue, a mosque, a secular humanist center, a communion that's a social movement, that's the engine of *The Universe: A Love Story* unfolding through us. Just as the Gospel Church was the engine for the civil rights movement and just as the Christian Church was the engine for moving out of the old world and into the beginning of the new, so too we founded this church to take us forward, to create tomorrow.

We begin with, always: *Hallelujah*. No bypass. We put everything on the altar. Remember *Hallelujah*? In Hebrew, *Hallelujah* means *hallel*, pristine praise, and *holelut*, drunken intoxication.

We come before the Divine, and we bring our holy and our broken *Hallelujah*, and we pray. Not to the ethnocentric, homophobic God, and not just to the God in me, but to the Infinity of Intimacy; to the arms of the Beloved that knows my name and cares about every detail of my life with infinite tenderness and quivering passion. As you pray, offer it up for the evolution of love.

THE POWER OF DEEPEST HEART'S DESIRE GROUPS

We are all members of the new species. We're all new humans, members of *Homo amor universalis*. We're members of this bigger church from all over the world participating in this evolutionary movement. Consider the first Pentecost when the disciples were able to hear in their own language, these Galileans, and then were able to go out and bless and heal and create a new world. We all have the power to bless the members of this new species in such a way that it helps us all take the next step after the Pentecost.

Feel into the planetary Pentecost, which is for people everywhere in the world like us who feel that they're emerging into greater love, greater creativity, greater wholeness, and who therefore, once they connect with each other in small groups—which we call deepest heart's desire groups— can join together with a purpose and a desire to help each other fulfill it.

We're seeing many small groups forming in the church, and elsewhere in the world, where people join together in their deepest heart's desire to create.

There's a certain methodology to deepest-heart's-desire groups for them to be successful. Everybody says exactly what they feel and then they get feedback, exactly what seems accurate. It's not *yes* or *no*, or *we agree* or *disagree*; but rather, when you hear each other, you're really listening to what this other person is wanting and needing and loving.

So, they get to be extremely caring of each other.

For the planetary awakening in love through a Unique Self Symphony, which is our shared goal of our church, we're wanting all our unique voices to be heard and woven together in a symphony. Each person's unique voice is heard and merges with others as everyone joins out of love.

Imagine what it feels like if people who are coming from love, coming from creativity, are joining in small groups to feel it? Because without that intimacy, you can't fully do it. The purpose of the small groups in the planetary awakening is intimacy, truthfulness, and caring.

I want to tell you something that happened to me (Barbara), about my own health. I didn't realize it, but I was having a lot of vibration in my body for weeks and weeks. I thought I was getting sick. The doctors couldn't find anything. Then, I was invited by wonderful people to join their deepest heart's desire group.

They just took me in and we began to talk, this direct intimacy, one-on-one, in such a loving way, and the next day the trembling in my body was gone and the aches in my body were gone.

I have a feeling that, as far as anyone is concerned, there's a deep longing for intimacy and shared experience and honesty and caring.

FEEL INTO THE EVER DEEPENING LOOPS OF INTIMACY

What does intimacy mean? Intimacy means something very specific. Let's talk about small groups. Intimacy means, always, shared identity.

Shared identity means is both a structure of how I understand myself, and that interior structure also has feeling. If we have a shared identity, then if your foot hurts, our foot hurts.

Shared identity means *feel me, feeling you*; that's the first loop of shared identity. We can actually feel each other; we have *empathos*. Not only is it *feel me, feeling you*, but we go to a second loop of intimacy which is *feel me, feeling you, feeling me*. Do you feel that?

- We start with just *feel me*. I feel you, and you feel me, loop one.
- Loop two is *feel me, feeling you*.
- Loop three is *feel me, feeling you, feeling me*.

When we feel each other, when we don't just *take* each other's perspective but *feel* each other's perspective, we create that intimacy of shared identity. At that moment, suffering ends on planet Earth because suffering is always a failure of intimacy.

Evil, at its core, is a failure of intimacy, which is why our core founding code in Evolutionary Church is, as always: *we live in a world of outrageous pain* (because outrageous pain is a failure of intimacy), *and the only response to outrageous pain is Outrageous Love.*

Outrageous Love is not ordinary love. It's not the strategy of the ego; it is Evolutionary Love, it's the love that initiates and animates Cosmos itself. To be an Outrageous Lover, an Evolutionary Lover, is to be one who participates in the restoration of intimacy, who participates in the evolution of love. What the evolution of intimacy means is, I can feel beyond myself. I feel beyond my own *pathos*. I feel beyond my own pride. I can genuinely feel your holy and broken *Hallelujah*. If you think about it from a Christian perspective, which emerged out of Isaiah, what do we mean when we say the *Divine is the Infinity of Intimacy*? It means the Divine doesn't need me in an obvious sense. It says, *I'm going to need you anyway.*

- God says, I'm going to need your service; I'm going to create a relationship in which I fall madly in love with you.
- Infinity says, I love finitude.
- Infinity says, I'm not going to be lost in the Infinity of Power. Infinity desires intimacy. Infinity loves intimacy.
- Infinity says, I'm going to need you, and I'm going to feel you.

The Christ idea, the Christ Consciousness, is that the Infinity of Intimacy says, *I feel every single person on the face of the planet, and I feel their holy and their broken Hallelujah.*

Right now, just take a moment and find a person who is outside of your circle of intimacy, because we all have people like that. Who's outside? Who have we left outside? Don't pick your obvious, archetypal enemy; it's too easy to bring them in. Pick the people we didn't notice, the people that we spoke to who were on our staff whose pain we didn't feel. Or the bank teller or the waiter, or the person I haven't called in twenty years, or the person with whom I'm insisting that I'm right.

Can I find that place where I open my heart again, and I bring someone into my circle of intimacy who doesn't feel good in my circle? How do I open my heart there? It's in that place where it happens. Let's feel it: intimacy is shared identity in the context of otherness. Can I expand my identity? Can I participate in the evolution of intimacy?

THE MOST PROFOUND PLEASURE IS THE PLEASURE OF TRANSFORMATION

Now that takes us to the core of our code. I want to talk about intimacy.

These are the political codes.

These are the economic codes.

These are the psychological codes.

This is a politics of Evolutionary Love. This is an evolution of the source code of culture, which is an evolution of love.

The reason we're in such pain is because we've lost our story.

Our colleague Yuval Harari, who wrote the books *Homo Deus* and *Sapiens*, recently gave a TED talk. He said, we have lost our way. We don't have a story. Sam Harris said, *so, tell us a new story*, and Yuval said, *wrong address, I don't do a new story.*

But we have to tell a new story. Something we've been talking about for the last seven years, every day, is to articulate the new story. **The new story, the new narrative, isn't a metaphor.**

It's the best integration of the deepest structures of meaning in exterior science, and interior science, and the premodern, modern, and postmodern period, woven together in a new configuration of intimacy, into a larger whole greater than the sum of the parts, just as da Vinci did at the dawn of the Renaissance.

Let's look at this code:

Reality is driven by pleasure.

What does that mean? It means that **evolution evolves because it feels good**; but we're not talking about an ice cream cone, as much as we like ice cream! Ice cream is awesome.

It feels good is an interior structure of Reality.

There's quantum hedonism: quarks come together because they're allured, and the interior quality of allurement is pleasure.

Reality is moved by Eros.

---

*Eros is the experience of radical aliveness
moving towards, desiring, ever deeper
contact and ever greater wholeness.*

But the interior feeling of Eros is pleasure. It's pleasure—and through discernment we clarify the true nature of pleasure—that drives Reality. Reality is driven by pleasure, number one.

Number two, what is the highest pleasure?

Let's say you're going to live forever. Let's say our friend Peter Diamandis has succeeded, and we're in the singularity. Here we are: immortality is happening now.

- We're taking 8,000 vitamins a day.
- We've become augmented cyborgs, and all the nanotech has worked.
- We've reconfigured and gene-spliced.
- We've done it all.
- We're going to live forever.

What's left? What's left is to grow. What's left is the pleasure of growing. **When we've done it all, the *only* pleasure that's left is the pleasure of transformation.**

Reality is driven by pleasure—that's the first part of the code. The second part is that *the highest pleasure is transformation.*

Now part three: What's the highest pleasure of transformation? Do you remember when Barack Obama ran for president? Why did Barack Obama run for president? What was he doing? He wanted to be president. Was it just for his ego? No! Was it just that he wanted to do good for people? Not quite. That doesn't quite move him twenty hours a day, for nine years, as president. What was driving him? If you watch Barack, you see one thing:

127

the dude is having a good time. It's pleasure! There's enormous pleasure in being president. Why? Well, because all a sudden everybody in the world knows you, but not in an egoic sense. It means that you can affect, touch, transform, move, evolve Reality. That's an incredible pleasure! That is not just Unique Self; it's what we call *Homo amor universalis*—it's Evolutionary Unique Self. **It's the realization that I can transform the whole thing**.

Let's look at the aspects of this code again:

- First, Reality is driven by pleasure from quantum hedonism, all the way up and all the way down. Reality is allurement-driven, animated by Eros, whose experience is pleasure, all the way up and all the way down.
- Second, the highest pleasure is the pleasure of transformation.
- Third, the highest pleasure of transformation is the experience that I can transform the whole thing. It's wild!

Let's say you don't have the Barack Obama option—you weren't born in the right place at the right time, you're not a senator from Illinois, and they have the Democratic nomination thing kind of sewed up. Running for Prime Minister in the Netherlands, that 's not going to work. France has a Prime Minister. What do you do? How do you participate in that pleasure? This is the core of the entire story. It's the core of Evolutionary Church; it's the core of everything.

When I awaken and I realize that:

- I'm a unique configuration of intimacy and desire.
- I'm a unique configuration of the evolutionary impulse awake and alive in me.
- I have a unique, personal transformation that can be done by me and me alone.

Once I realize this, something profoundly pleasurable happens.

When I realize that there's a unique, personal transformation that's mine to do, and mine alone, and then I realize that my unique, personal transformation—which is what evolution desires and desperately needs from me and me alone, that can be done by no one who ever was, is, or will be other than me—**my unique personal transformation transforms the entire thing, I experience the most profound pleasure possible.**

Oh my God! It's not a metaphor; it's ontology. That's the nature of Reality!

TRANSFORMATION IS ALWAYS TO EVOLVE MY CAPACITY FOR INTIMACY

The unique, personal transformation that's mine to do and mine alone by definition, structurally, transforms the entire field because there's no local desire; there's no local transformation; there's a quantum field; there's a field of transformation.

Now let's put it together. How does the *intimacy* code connect to the *transformation* code? It's so gorgeous, it's so beautiful, and it just makes you cry because beauty is truth and truth is beauty.

My personal transformation is always to evolve my capacity for intimacy.

That's always what it is. It's always to find the edge of my discomfort, the place where I can't get intimate. Either I'm split off from a part of myself—in which case to be intimate is to be intimate with all of my parts and all of the voices in me—or I'm split off from a person who should be in my circle of intimacy and influence, or I'm split off from a set of my unique gifts.

When I meet the edge of my capacity for intimacy, and I awaken, and I extend that capacity:

- I open my heart again.
- I expand my circle of intimacy to include more of myself.
- I expand more of my circle of intimacy to include people who

129

don't feel right to me and don't aesthetically please me in the way that I'd like my circle of intimacy to look like.

- I can break my heart open again and again to evolve the unique circle of intimacy, which is the unique configuration of my life.

When I do that, that *is* my personal unique transformation.

That transformation participates directly in the evolution of intimacy.

I affect the whole because I am intimacy, I am transformation.

When I know that's true, when I feel it in the depths of my heart, then, oh my God, everything changes.

I am intimacy. I am transformation.

When we say that, then we become love in action, and we become intimacy in action.

CHAPTER TEN

FROM HOMO ARMOR TO HOMO AMOR: RADICAL CURIOSITY AND PERSONAL TRANSFORMATION

Episode 110 — November 24, 2018

EVOLUTIONARY LOVE CODE: THE HIGHEST PLEASURE IS TRANSFORMATION

Reality is driven by pleasure.

The highest pleasure is transformation.

Every human being is born to effect a unique personal transformation. Every human being is born to effect a unique social transformation.

Wisdom is knowing what is yours to transform and what is not. The highest pleasure is the transformation of everything.

The highest "knowing" is to know that your radical commitment to your unique transformation is what transforms everything.

LOVE AND CURIOSITY GO TOGETHER

Lots of times, during holidays like Thanksgiving in North America, we get together not with what I would call

our *evolutionary friends*, but with our *historical friends*, or our *historical family*. Sometimes, if we're blessed in this incarnation, our family is our evolutionary pod: it's with my family where I can do my highest transformation and have my highest experience. I can be in the most subtle place, the most curious place of listening to each other, of impacting each other and transforming.

Sometimes my family is my historical family. This is the family I was born into, that Reality brought me together with. These are the people that I came together with. It's not the place where I can do certain kinds of high transformation, but one where we hold each other, and we love each other in other ways. Thanksgiving, for example, is a time when these different kinds of relationships come together in this new way, and we feel each other in these different places.

People often ask me, *where do Evolutionary Love Codes come from?* We are creating an entire new set of Evolutionary Love Codes. For example, the code above—I have been thinking about that code for thirty years. It's not cute. It is not clever. It's like, *you're in.*

For me, my personal transformation is to go so clean and so deep into myself that I can become a clear vessel to try to access the codes of Reality, and share them, so that we have a new source code, going forward.

To do it, you don't just read a book. What it means is that you're always curious. Last night I (Marc) was thinking, reading, trying to formulate it until about 1 a.m. I got up a few hours later and happened to be, without exaggeration, in an eighteen-hour day, in *code mode*, trying to clarify codes. Like anything, all greatness—whether it's soccer or conscious evolution— whatever it is, comes from the delight of radical commitment.

I want to invite you to **find the place in your life where you are radically committed.** That's the first thing. The thing I have most gratitude for is that I'm radically committed, which is a gift from Goddess. When I say *I*, I mean *Goddess living in me, She living in me, Reality flowing through me. I am radically committed.*

132

The second gift that She gives me is, and I want to ask you to find this, the fact that *I'm radically curious.*

One of my deep rules that I have when I'm in a conversation with someone is that I want to get curious about what they say. So, if they say something, I want to feed back to them, *oh, I got it*, and then I want to be more curious.

I don't want to be right.
I want to be curious.

Love and curiosity go together. Curious means, *I want to know how you feel*. How do you feel? Sometimes we don't get it, so we have to listen even more deeply.

We call that *pathos* or *empathos,* which is the core to intimacy in our codes: Intimacy is shared identity. Intimacy is *feel me feeling you. Feel you, feeling me.* When I'm curious I want to be radically curious about you.

What does it feel like for my close beloveds to be traveling in their world? They're having feelings and experiences. How do I get out of my own local experience? What is it like for my friends to be doing what they do? What is their experience of life? We get curious with each other. A world with curiosity is a world with love. The second we stop being curious about each other's experience, we lose love. Feel that nexus between love and curiosity.

Just this morning before church, I had a conversation with someone and I felt like I was receiving, but I couldn't find them. I got a little closed at first, and then I got curious. *Oh! Oh! Oh! Let me get out of myself. What's your experience? What's it like ? Where are you sitting? What's going on for you?*

The second I get curious, my heart opens.

We've kind of relegated curiosity to a monkey named George. Remember Curious George? My son loved Curious George! From the ages of four to seven, he would make me read Curious George again and again. Curious George is actually our spiritual master!

Curious George is curious, and he gets into all sorts of trouble. So, I just want to invite Curious George into Evolutionary Church, and we can access that part of ourselves: *I am curious*. When I'm curious about someone, I get a feeling for how they're going to react because I can feel into their space.

Curiosity is connected to intimacy.

GREATNESS MEANS TO MAKE NEW MISTAKES

The highest transformation is the transformation of everything. That is the third part of the code:

> Pleasure is the interior feeling of Eros. Reality is Pleasure. **Evolution evolves because it *feels good*.**

But "feel good" is in quotation marks. When I write Feel Good, it's capital F, capital G. Feel Good! Feel Good is the deepest structure of Reality. Feeling Good is not easy. A Baby Ruth chocolate bar feels good! But does it? When you check out Feel Good, you have to check out the *depth of the feeling*. Great wine feels good, if you're a connoisseur. Knowing what feels good, cultivating Feel Good is the highest level of evolutionary development.

The highest level of pleasure is the pleasure of transformation. The highest pleasure of transformation is when you can transform the whole thing. But how do you transform the whole thing? **You transform the whole thing through your unique personal transformation**. I want to invite us to pray to know our own, unique, personal transformation.

We think our transformation is someplace else. I think my transformation is in this, or in that. But, actually, my transformation might be in an entirely different place. In other words, I think that *I need to be functional and effective and get it done*. But maybe my transformation is in places where I have contracted to the people closest to me—because we all have our circle of intimacy—and I need to blow my circle away with my open heart.

Or maybe I think I need to blow my circle away with my open heart, but I need to get more functional and more reliable. Whatever you think your *default* is:

Usually, our default is the place where we don't need to transform.

Don't lose your default, your default is fantastic. It's your gorgeous, beautiful, natural expression of your ebullient, effervescent, perspicacious, non-mendacious, spacious, obviously loquacious self!

The place where your default is competent or good, whatever your default is, keep it. Keep your gorgeous default but notice that your default usually moves you away. It's a decoy, sometimes, so you can't see the place where you can transform. If you can see the place where you can transform, you can change everything.

I want to give you just one example, then we'll pray. I want to invite you to bring this into prayer: we bring our holy and our broken *Hallelujah,* with Leonard Cohen's song, which means we're going to bring the entire story of our lives, the holy and the broken *Hallelujah*, our blown open hearts, our devastation, and our hurt, and our pain. We're going to bring it all and offer it up to God.

The god you don't believe in doesn't exist. We turn toward the God who is the Infinity of Intimacy, who knows our name. First, ask for what you need personally, for what your friends need, your family, what the world needs. Ask for everything.

Second, I want to invite a particular kind of prayer which is to ask the Divine, the Infinity of Intimacy, to ask yourself:

Could I be intimate enough with myself to know what my unique transformation is? Can I be intimate enough with myself to feel how I'm showing up in the world and where that unique point of transformation is?

I'm just going to give you an example, then let's pray. Here's my Bill Clinton example.

Bill Clinton thinks, *Man, I'm awesome!* And he is. He's awesome. *I'm super smart; I care about people enormously, and I'm really creative, and I am unbelievably strategic.* Great dude!

But then Bill has got this thing, he's a little bit promiscuous-impulsive. He has an impulsive promiscuity. Not just that he loves people, but that he's not discerning. Bill, man, what are you hanging out with that intern for? Bad idea!

Now, not a bad idea if you have worked it out with Hillary so that it is totally beautiful, and she loves Monica—awesome! But it's just not working, man. You're the president; she's hanging out with people. You don't have a formal covenant with her. You haven't worked this out; you haven't created a space for her to talk to other people. You haven't created any kind of Holy of Holies.

This is kind of a little loose and sloppy, buddy. And you're the president! You can pass healthcare; you can affect millions of lives. But you have got this little default thing that you keep doing.

Bill, you actually caused us an Iraq war because Al Gore didn't want you to campaign for him. He won the election by the popular vote but lost the electoral vote. Had you been able to campaign, and you had not had this compulsive promiscuity, we wouldn't have had an Iraq war!

We default to what we're good at, and we forget that there's a unique point of transformation.

That unique point of transformation is a big deal! It's everything! That's where greatness happens. A great person is not a person who is publicly successful. You can be publicly successful and be a flaming mistake. But your greatness means you make new mistakes.

Greatness means I step out of my pattern, and I make a new mistake. That's a big deal.

My interior point of transformation transforms everything. It's not a metaphor, this code. Codes are never metaphors. If Goddess graces us, codes are the ontological structure and source code of Reality itself. **An Evolutionary Love Code is the great physics of the interior face of the Cosmos.** That idea, that my interior point of transformation transforms everything—wow, that's powerful!

We're evolving the source code. We're at the abyss, standing, saying, *Let there be light.* We're the response to the dissolution. It's our turn. We're what we've been waiting for. We're honored and delighted to be together.

GO THE WHOLE WAY IN YOUR RADICAL TRANSFORMATION

I've prayed to go the whole way in this lifetime. I've imagined what the whole way in this lifetime is, since, in this lifetime, it appears that evolution itself is shifting from the path that could destroy life towards this new path, the crisis of birth for a new humanity.

Anybody who wants to go the whole way in this lifetime as part of your unique gift, has to be prepared for radical newness.

Can you fathom the depths of this code? If Reality is driven by pleasure, and God drives Reality, then *God is driven by pleasure.* What is God's highest pleasure? It's the radical transformation of everything, including you, and me, and us. So, really, **God is on our side here.** God's intention is that Reality be pleasurable, and pleasure is transformation.

Let's look at that more closely: is pleasure transformation? Is your greatest pleasure transformation? Here's how I think that is so. It goes to another, deeper code that we've developed, which is that **Reality is the evolution of intimacy.**

Evolution creates newness through intimacy, through connecting separate parts together to make a new whole. So, if we're really driven by pleasure and the highest pleasure is transformation then, in order to transform uniquely, we need to be connected more deeply in intimacy with each other. That's key: to connect more deeply in intimacy with each other. How do we connect more deeply in intimacy, and with whom, and how?

We were saying above that Bill Clinton made some mistakes, in a very *superficial way*, in connecting in intimacy. For radical transformation to occur, which is pleasurable, we can only do it by connecting *more deeply* in intimacy.

We've talked about joining genius as the way we create the new human. *Joining genius* is not joining intimately with just anybody, even though you might like many people. Since God is driven by pleasure and pleasure comes through transformation which happens through increased intimacy, **to have the full pleasure of Reality, you need to experience deep intimacy**

with the person whose genius is closest to your own. That person is someone who, when you are intimately joining genius with them, you begin to fulfill pleasure, transformation, and your deepest heart's desire. Isn't that a good plan that God has given us? God has given us the plan, yes! Wow!

Let's focus on your deepest drive for Reality that comes through your transformation and your pleasure. Your pleasure and transformation come through increased intimacy, to make a greater whole that's greater than the sum of your parts.

Imagine joining in the pleasure of profound intimacy—with the one, or ones, with whom, when we join genius, each of us becomes *Homo amor universalis*. It may well be that the new human cannot happen without joining genius, just as new babies can't happen without us joining genes in love.

FROM *HOMO ARMOR* TO *HOMO AMOR*

Can I love myself so madly that I move from *Homo armor* to *Homo amor*?

To be armored means I'm not curious. I can't be curious because I'm armored. Armored means I have to be right in some way. I can't let my armor open. **The place where my armor opens is always the place where it's uncomfortable.**

I (Marc) remember that I went to this place where a very close friend of mine is the Reverend, and my heart was blown open. There were a few thousand of us, one Sunday morning. Right after church I started hanging out with my friend and talking to the different people in church. Very quickly I realized that the church itself, right underneath the thin veneer of New Age delight—and it can be a fundamentalist delight or a New Age delight or an evolutionary delight—was filled with backbiting and politics and agendas. No one could give up being right, and no one was curious about each other.

139

One of the things we try really hard to do in the worlds of the Center for Integral Wisdom, Evolutionary Church, and the Foundation for Conscious Evolution, is to ensure that the inside and the outside are the same, that we are not doing this surface, commodified selling of Spirit. We're madly loving each other.

To madly love each other is not always easy. A mad love story is the agony and the ecstasy.

It means that we're opening our hearts again and again, and we're willing to go to that uncomfortable place and melt our hearts again.

We did a board meeting at our friend John Mackey's ranch a couple of years ago, and there were about seventy-five people there, leaders from all over the country. I would say we were there for about four days. There wasn't a drop of politics for four days. People were deeply loving each other, but not on the surface. We were working stuff out. There were a million things that needed to be worked out. There's always stuff to work out!

- Can I get curious enough to find the place in myself that's too soft, and should get fierce, or the place in myself that's too hard, that's closed, that's locked in an old pattern, that's not in the present?
- Can I get curious enough to find that place in myself that's locked in the default mode network of the brain, that's rooted in my relationship to my father that I thought I had worked out, but hadn't; or my relationship to my mother, where I thought I had gotten over the pain of my mother's semi-indifference to me, and I didn't learn how to take love in, in a real way?
- Can I get curious enough to find that place where I keep re-enacting the same pattern again and again so I can't actually be intimate?

We don't get stuck there. It's not that we spend our lives in the circle—we transform it in the way that we can. If I can say what Evolutionary Church is, it's that we're participating together in evolving the source code and awakening as Outrageous Lovers but, part of our transformation is that we're bringing together this deep attention and curiosity to *where is the point of my personal breakthrough?*

Let me (Marc) model it myself. I will give you a personal breakthrough of mine. I have an enormous fear around money. I grew up poor. In my family if you took an extra piece of cheese, you got into trouble. I remember getting in big trouble with my mother for taking an extra piece of cheese.

I grew up with a sense of radical vulnerability because my mother is a Holocaust survivor. It's a bad set of stories. We're not going to go into them now, but she was buried alive, she was in front of a firing squad, and I grew up with this enormously painful experience that you can be friends with everyone and then, all of a sudden, there's this new political structure, you're betrayed and six million people are dead. I lost almost my entire family in the Holocaust, and my mother always said to me, *it's your job to make sure Hitler lost.* Nice thing to say to a kid!

My mother is awesome, but it's kind of a heavy burden, if you get what I mean. I grew up with two things. First, I grew up with a vulnerability and an enormous pain about betrayal because my mother told me, day and night, stories about betrayal; and second, I grew up with an enormous sense of financial vulnerability.

For example, this week a very close friend of mine who's been with me for years, and is going to be with me for years, had to reconfigure something about their support of the Center and it went through my body as a fear, a very deep financial fear. That's kind of wild!

I realized both that it was real, that it had a basis in Reality, *and* it was also old. It was both. It was both true and yet the trauma was old. I had to love my way through the fear. I had to find my way out. For about a day,

I couldn't open my heart. That person is gorgeous and awesome—it has nothing to do with that person—but they triggered it in me.

Two things that I watch for in my life: first, loyalty is very important—not a blind, mafia loyalty, but a higher, second-tier loyalty. I watch for whether people have loyalty as a value. That's a big trigger for me. Second, finances are also a big trigger. The reason I'm offering a personal example is, without making it personal, it's not real.

Everybody's got stuff.

- It might be impulsivity.
- It might be that I can't feel the field.
- It might be I don't know how to transmit my love to places where my love is needed, to hold the energy of a space.
- It might be that I get contracted and I have a *lies and excuses file* that always makes me right.

Everyone has a way of strategizing this; no one's an exception. There's not one person here, not one of us, who doesn't have some version of what I just said.

If I just say, *I'm going to write the dharma*, but I don't go into the personal place where something in me is broken, and I don't do that work, then something is off. Ramana Maharshi, the great, realized Ramana Maharshi had *stuff* with his mother. How do I know? Because I know! He used to come to me for therapy. That's not true—I made that up! Do you get what I'm saying though? Moses had stuff going on. Jesus had to work out his relationship with Mary Magdalene, and then there was the Judas problem. There's always stuff.

Don't get lost in the stuff; be curious! **Turn to that place where *I can transform*, where I work with that place of brokenness in me, and I break it open without—and here is the key—*freeze-framing* there, without getting stuck there.**

> *Getting addicted to always working with my wound is its own form of addiction.*

What I mean by not getting stuck is that when I'm out there, when I'm transforming, my focus is, *what can I give, how can I serve?* I'm in full powerful devotion. I'm not trapped in what Christina Hoff Sommers calls the *therapeutic culture* where my work with my wound becomes the sum total of my life. No, it's one piece.

Part of the gorgeous move in the evolution of the source code of culture that we're making here in Evolutionary Church is:

- We're radical activists
- We're evolving the source code.
- We're radically committed to personal transformation.

This is where the code comes together.

My personal transformation with evolutionary intention participates, literally, ontologically, in the transformation of the whole thing.

This is not made up. It's not a metaphor.

This is actually how it works.

My personal transformation is not an accident; it's not by chance.

It was the choice of an intentional Cosmos that created the web structure of my life for me to be invited into this particular moment of transformation.

APPENDIX: SONGS

THE BATTLE HYMN OF THE REPUBLIC— JULIA WARD HOWE[1]

Mine eyes have seen the glory of the coming
of the Lord.

He has trampled down the vintage
where the grapes of wrath are stored.

He has loosed the fateful lightning
of his terrible swift sword.

His truth is marching on.

HOW COULD ANYONE—LIBBY RODERICK[2]

How could anyone ever tell you
you were anything less than beautiful?

How could anyone ever tell you
you were less than whole?

How could anyone fail to notice
that your loving is a miracle—
how deeply you're connected to my soul?

---

1 Julia Ward Howe, The Battle Hymn of the Republic, 1862.
2 Libby Roderick, "How Could Anyone," on *If You See a Dream* (Turtle Island Records, 1990), CD.

I WANT TO KNOW WHAT LOVE IS—FOREIGNER[3]

I've gotta take a little time,
a little time to think things over.
I better read between the lines,
in case I need it when I'm older.
(Whoa, ooh-ooh, ooh-ooh)

And this mountain, I must climb
feels like the world upon my shoulders,
and through the clouds, I see love shine,
it keeps me warm as life grows colder.

[Pre-Chorus]
In my life, there's been heartache and pain.
I don't know if I can face it again.
Can't stop now, I've travelled so far
to change this lonely life.

[Chorus]
I wanna know what love is.
I want you to show me.
I wanna feel what love is.
I know you can show me.
Oh, oh-oh, oh (ooh)

I'm gonna take a little time,
a little time to look around me.
I've got nowhere left to hide,
it looks like love has finally found me.

[Pre-Chorus]

[Chorus]

[Outro]

(And I wanna feel) I wanna feel what love is

---

3 Foreigner, "I Want to Know What Love Is," recorded November 1984, on *Agent Provocateur*, Atlantic Records, vinyl LP.

(And I know) I know you can show me.
Let's talk about love.
(I wanna know what love is) The love that you feel inside.
(I want you to show me) And I'm feelin' so much love.
(I wanna feel what love is) No, you just cannot hide.
(I know you can show me) Yeah.
I wanna know what love is (Let's talk about love).
I want you to show me, I wanna feel.
(I wanna feel what love is) And I know, and I know.
I know you can show me (Yeah).
(I wanna know what love is) (I wanna know)
(I want you to show me) I wanna know, I wanna know, wanna know.
(I wanna feel what love is) (I wanna feel)
(I know you can show me).

HALLELUJAH—LEONARD COHEN[4]

Now, I've heard there was a secret chord
that David played, and it pleased the Lord.
But you don't really care for music, do you?
It goes like this, the fourth, the fifth,
the minor fall, the major lift.
The baffled king composing Hallelujah.

[Chorus]

Hallelujah, Hallelujah,
Hallelujah, Hallelujah.

Your faith was strong, but you needed proof.
You saw her bathing on the roof.
Her beauty and the moonlight overthrew you.
She tied you to a kitchen chair,
she broke your throne, and she cut your hair,
and from your lips she drew the Hallelujah.

---

4 Leonard Cohen, "Hallelujah", *Various Positions*, Columbia Records, 1984, LP.

[Chorus]

You say I took the name in vain,
I don't even know the name,
but if I did, well, really, what's it to you?
There's a blaze of light in every word,
it doesn't matter which you heard,
the holy or the broken Hallelujah.

[Chorus]

I did my best, it wasn't much.
I couldn't feel, so I tried to touch.
I've told the truth, I didn't come to fool you.
And even though it all went wrong,
I'll stand before the Lord of Song
With nothing on my tongue but Hallelujah.

OM NAMAH SHIVAAYA

Om Namah Shivaaya
Shivaaya namaha,
Shivaaya namah om
Shivaaya namaha, namaha Shivaaya
Shambhu Shankara namah Shivaaya,
Girijaa Shankara namah Shivaaya
Arunaachala Shiva namah Shivaaya

*I bow to the soul of all. I bow to my Self. I don't know who I am,
so I bow to you, Shiva, my own true Self. I bow to my teachers
who loved me with love. Who took care of me when I couldn't
take care of myself. I owe everything to them. How can I repay
them? They have everything in the world. Only my love is mine
to give, but in giving I find that it is their love flowing through
me back to the world…I have nothing. I have everything. I want
nothing. Only let it flow to you, my love… sing!*

147

INDEX

embracing, 47, 92

emerge, 7, 8, 9, 10, 11, 27, 50, 65, 67, 92, 112, 113, 122, 124

empathos, 124, 133

empower, 35, 36

emptiness, 70, 102

enlightenment, 21, 52, 66, 70, 100

Eros, 1, 8, 39, 40, 50, 67, 74, 78, 109, 126, 127, 128, 134

ethnocentric, 32, 91, 98, 121, 122

ever-deeper, 76, 126

ever-greater, 35, 126

evil, 33, 124

evolution, 2, 7, 8, 9, 10, 16, 17, 22, 23, 24, 31, 34, 35, 37, 40, 41, 44, 47, 49, 50, 55, 61, 69, 80, 82, 84, 85, 90, 92, 93, 94, 96, 97, 99, 101, 108, 113, 114, 115, 117, 118, 119, 120, 122, 124, 125, 126, 127, 128, 129, 130, 134, 137, 138, 140, 143
    of intimacy, 2, 7, 50, 115, 117, 120, 124, 125, 130, 138
    of love, 7, 22, 47, 61, 69, 82, 90, 92, 115, 119, 120, 122, 124, 125

Evolutionary
    Church, 2, 4, 6, 8, 17, 23, 24, 32, 35, 36, 41, 42, 48, 76, 80, 82, 89, 90, 92, 94, 97, 100, 106, 107, 108, 111, 116, 120, 124, 128, 134, 139, 140, 143
    impulse, 10, 22, 24, 50, 128
    Love, 4, 22, 23, 24, 35, 37, 39, 42, 54, 73, 80, 83, 87, 97, 108, 116, 117, 120, 124, 132, 137
    Love Code, 37, 73, 87, 116, 132, 137
    Unique Self, 28, 36, 41, 108, 128

Evolutionary Love, 90, 125

Evolutionary Love Code, 132, 137

exile, 27, 102

existential risk, 3

expand, 8, 120, 125, 129

Eye
    of humanity, 9, 24, 81, 82, 92, 97, 112, 113
    of Spirit, 19, 55, 74, 75, 92, 117, 139

F

face, 32, 68, 90, 97, 106, 125, 137

faith, 94, 114

father, 52, 95, 140

features, 1, 4, 15, 25

feelings, 3, 10, 11, 17, 21, 37, 54, 77, 113, 114, 118, 123, 124, 127, 133, 134

field, 2, 4, 5, 6, 9, 18, 27, 28, 29, 56, 129

Field of Desire, 2, 11, 25, 29

first person, 19

forgive, 80, 81, 117

freedom, 33, 35

fulfilment, 35, 95

fundamental, 26, 27

fundamentalism, 91, 97

fundamentalist, 6, 92, 97, 139

G

Garden of Eden, 99

genius, 22, 24, 48, 114, 118, 138, 139

gifts, 29, 34, 65, 66, 67, 132, 133

Global
    intimacy, 50, 75, 76, 91

ABOUT THE AUTHORS

Dr. Marc Gafni is a visionary world philosopher and futurist, one of the leading formulators of world spirituality and religion of our time, and a beloved teacher and public intellectual. He holds his doctorate in philosophy from Oxford University, as well as Orthodox rabbinic ordination. He co-founded the activist think tank, now called the Center for World Philosophy and Religion where he serves as the co-president with Dr. Zachary Stein. He also served with Barbara Marx Hubbard as co-president of the Foundation for Conscious Evolution, which he consented to lead at Barbara's request after her passing.

He is known for his "source code teachings"—including Unique Self theory and the Five Selves, the Amorous Cosmos, a Politics of Evolutionary Love, a Return to Eros, and Digital Intimacy—and has more than twenty books to his name, including the award-winning Your Unique Self, A Return to Eros, and three volumes of Radical Kabbalah.

He teaches on the cutting edge of philosophy in the West, helping to evolve a new "*dharma*" or meta-theory of Integral meaning that is helping to re-shape key pivoting points in global consciousness and culture, with the aim of participating in the articulation of what Dr. Gafni together with Dr. Stein and colleagues are calling CosmoErotic Humanism.

At the core of CosmoErotic Humanism is what Dr. Gafni and Dr. Stein are calling First Principles and First Values, Anthro-Ontology, and a Universal Grammar of Value. This is the ground of a new shared universe story and a new narrative of identity for the new human and the new humanity. This is what they are calling the emergence from Homo sapiens to Homo Amor.

This shared story rooted in First Principles and First Values can then serve as the matrix for a global ethos for a global civilization.

Together with Dr. Stein and Ken Wilber, Gafni is writing a series of seminal books under the collective pseudonym of David J. Temple, which intend to evolve the source code of consciousness and culture in response to the meta-crisis. The first of those books is *First Principles and First Values: Forty-Two Propositions on CosmoErotic Humanism, the Meta-Crisis, and the World to Come.*

Barbara Marx Hubbard (born Barbara Marx; December 22, 1929–April 10, 2019) was an American futurist, author, and public speaker. She is credited with the Wheel of Co-Creation and together with Dr. Gafni, the Wheel of Co-Creation 2.0, as well as the concepts of the Synergy Engine and the "birthing" of humanity.

As co-founder and president of the Foundation for Conscious Evolution and the chair, for the last five years of her life, of the Center for World Philosophy and Religion, she posited that humanity was on the threshold of a quantum leap if newly emergent scientific, social, and spiritual capacities were integrated to address global crises.

She was the author of seven books on social and planetary evolution. In conjunction with the Shift Network, she co-produced the worldwide "Birth 2012" multimedia event. She was also the subject of a biography by author Neale Donald Walsch, *The Mother of Invention: The Legacy of Barbara Marx Hubbard*. Deepak Chopra called her "the voice for conscious evolution."

In 1984, she was symbolically nominated for the vice presidency of the United States. She also co-chaired a number of Soviet-American Citizen Summits, introducing a new concept called SYNCON, to foster synergistic convergence with opposing groups. In addition, she co-founded the World Future Society and the Association for Global New Thought.

Voolume 11 — The Evolution of Intimacy

LIST OF EPISODES

www.ingramcontent.com/pod-product-compliance
Lightning Source LLC
LaVergne TN
LVHW011156080426
835508LV00007B/439